FULLY HUMAN

WHY THE HUMANITY OF JESUS CHANGES
EVERYTHING

GREG HAUGH

Printed in the United States of America

Edited by Andrew Kroeger and Elijah Dove

Published by Barton Hill Books

www.bartonhillbooks.com

ISBN: 978-0-9996372-1-0

CONTENTS

Dedication   v

Preface   ix

Introduction   1

PART I
JESUS LIVING AS A HUMAN: EMBRACING A
DOWNWARD TRAJECTORY

1. Not a Superhero   5

2. Emptied Out   11

3. A Shady Birth   17

4. Human Limitations   23

5. Temptations   31

6. The Power of Touch   37

7. Tears of Compassion   49

8. The Rejection of Jesus   57

9. Foot Washing   63

10. Keeping It Together in Gethsemane   69

11. Forsaken   75

PART II
THE NEW CHRISTIAN OBSESSION: CHASING
AN UPWARD TRAJECTORY

12. Slaves to the American Dream   83

13. Big-Face Worship   97

14. Happiness Versus Joy   105

15. The Advantages of Being Disadvantaged   115

16. Conclusion: What Would Jesus Think of Us?   131

Notes   139

About the Author   143

Thanks for reading!   145

DEDICATION

This book is dedicated to all the people who have helped me walk through all the pain and suffering during my life, as well as those who have helped me appreciate the little things that we so often miss along the way:

- To my younger brother Jono for teaching us to appreciate the simple things of life and giving us all a huge sense of compassion and empathy towards others
- To my parents, my brother Nate, and my sister Caralyn for your unwavering love and support through all the ups and downs of life, even when it seemed like what I was doing was crazy
- To my wife Melanie for your love, support, and encouragement in the midst of two difficult but good years of marriage
- To Uncle Mike for loving, supporting, and

encouraging me like your own son from the night I was born until now

- To (the fellas) Huy Do, Brent Zakaryan, Mark Saukkola, Mike Bair, Casey Chop, Tim Fitzpatrick, Mike Modeer, and Alec Dressel for your love and support that leaves me blown away by how many *brothers* God has given me. I love you all like brothers, and I wouldn't be here today without your love, support, and encouragement over the years

- To all my in-laws for helping me appreciate the simple things like wine, cheese, crackers, good food, classical music, and sharing time with family and friends

- To Bill and Chris Welch for your guidance, wisdom, counsel, and encouragement for Melanie and I; and for helping me through the stuff I was going through that led to Part II of this book

- To Doug Clarkson for spending countless hours meeting with me at Del Taco, helping me through the ups and downs, so I could develop into the person I am today

- To the people of Latin America who I love like my own family, and where I spent six and a half years, for teaching me to appreciate the little things in life and to value spending time with people. You taught me how to depend on God and break through the shallow appearances that far too much of my country and culture are based on. ¡Te amo mucho!

The King came down
Wouldn't grasp equality,
Left his station...and his crown
To search for you and me
The broken-hearted...and Esteemed,
The good, bad, the in-between.

The Spirit reaches down
As far as you and me,
Then moves on to other ground
And places seldom seen,
In the ashes...on the streets,
Among the ruins...so complete.

Now...who will go down with them?
Embrace lowliness today?
Leave his station...or her crown
For those out of the way.
Or will we grasp our standing
In the house we build today,
And find he's moving down the road,
seeking those who could not pray?
—Terry Haugh

PREFACE

Part I of this book was based on a series of blog posts, called "Fully Human," that I wrote years ago for someone else's blog. But the original blog series was based on a teaching series, called "Fully Human: The Humanity of Jesus," I did while I was the College and Young Adult Director at Christ Pacific Church from 2007 to 2010 in Huntington Beach.

I adapted those blog posts into what you have in Part I of this book, but have greatly expanded upon them. I also included a couple of chapters that were not in the original blog series, but which were part of the teaching series I did at CPC.

I am deeply indebted to my good friend and mentor Bill Welch for the content in Part II. Bill and his wife Chris did pre-marriage counseling with Melanie and I, and they have also been invaluable mentors and rocks for us to turn to during our first two years of marriage.

Bill also gave me the book I use in Part II to talk about how our perspectives change when we suffer from disabilities. As you read Part II, this will all make sense to you. I am eternally grateful to Bill and Chris for their constant love, support, and guidance as we all walk through the tough and unpredictable roads of life.

As always, I am also greatly indebted to Andrew Kroeger and his team at Barton Hill Books. Without Andrew's constant encouragement, wisdom, advice, suggestions, expertise, and, most importantly, belief in this book, it simply never would have become a reality. I love working with you, and I don't take for granted the fact that I have absolute trust in you when it comes to the whole process of writing, editing, and shaping books together. Here's to many more books in the future!

INTRODUCTION

Welcome! I want to thank you for reading this book. It is a book about the humanity of Jesus, but as you will see, it also has huge implications for how we live our lives. The main point I will make in this book is that the downward trajectory of the life of Jesus contradicts our modern obsession with upward trajectory and motion in our lives.

As American Christians, we have built our faiths, lives, churches, and ministries upon an obsession with moving always upward. We obsess with obtaining more of whatever we have, and often we will do almost anything to get it. But that contradicts the downward motion and trajectory of Jesus. In this book we will lay out each of these main points to see how Jesus lived, and then I will try to point us forward in his footsteps so we learn to follow him and not our culture.

I

JESUS LIVING AS A HUMAN: EMBRACING A DOWNWARD TRAJECTORY

1

NOT A SUPERHERO

We see it in so many movies: a superhero runs into a burning building, clad in a super-suit that grants him special powers, guaranteeing his safety. Crowds marvel at the superhero's apparent bravery and courage, but, in reality, there wouldn't be much to admire as the superhero was never in any danger.

Although this may be an odd way to think about the humanity of Jesus, I think the same basic principle applies. Let me explain.

I've always assumed that if there is a God, then there's also a reasonable expectation that God would attempt to communicate with us about himself, his will for us, and the purpose of our existence.

After all, why would God go through all the trouble of creating anything at all if he refused to interact or relate to his creation in any way? To me, if creation exists (which it obviously does), and God exists (which I believe), then I would expect God to try to communicate with us *in some way*. So I'm not surprised in the least bit that God tried to communicate with us, or come to us in one way or another.

But what blows my mind is when I think about the *particular way* God chose to come to us in the person of Jesus Christ: as fully, totally, utterly, and beautifully human.

It is Jesus's raw humanness that compels me to fall on my knees and commit my life to him; for in Jesus's humanity, I see just how low God was willing to stoop, how far he was willing to reach, and how much he was willing to suffer in order to reach and save us.

Most American Christians today focus so much on Jesus's divinity that we almost completely disregard his humanity. For example, in most of our images of Jesus, there's always a magic glowing light shining just behind his head that presumably followed him wherever he went. Or he is shown with a glowing heart that is nothing like our human hearts, but both of these are supposed to draw our attention to the fact that Jesus was divine.

Now, I believe Jesus was divine, but I don't believe he had a spotlight that followed him around, or that his heart actually glowed like so many of the images we use when we think about him; but that's my point.

We don't expect to see normal human beings who are followed around by a glowing light or who have glowing hearts, because we know we're all human beings and not divine. But we don't question these ridiculous and unrealistic images when they apply to Jesus, because we have been so trained to accept his divinity in those kinds of strange ways.

This is the same reason we imagine baby Jesus as a serene infant who never cried, when the truth is that all human babies cry, and therefore Jesus must have cried, too. Most Christians think of the attributes of God as all-knowing and all-powerful (however you define those terms) and apply them directly to Jesus.

When we do this, we understand Jesus as if his humanity didn't exist or wasn't real.

That's why we're uncomfortable thinking about Jesus going to the bathroom, getting sick, puking, having zits as a teenager, or banging his finger with his hammer while he was working. And yet, as all normal human beings do those things, Jesus surely did them at one time or another.

This is also why most Christians overlook passages that state or imply there were things Jesus didn't know, like the time of his own return,[1] who touched his robe,[2] or whether or not his father could take away his cup of suffering.[3]

He also *"increased in wisdom,"* revealing again that he didn't know everything.[4] After all, how can someone who knows everything increase in wisdom? That's impossible, which implies there were things Jesus didn't know.

Other scriptural passages Christians tend to overlook imply Jesus was not all-powerful: *"he could not do any miracles"* due to the lack of peoples' faith in his own hometown.[5] This is why renowned New Testament scholar Dr. Craig Evans says this about these incorrect beliefs of most American Christians:

> Personally, I think a lot of Christians—even conservative Bible believing Christians—are semi-docetic. . . . They halfway believe—without ever giving it any serious thought . . . that Jesus actually wasn't real. 'Oh, yes, of course, he's real,' they'll say. But they're not entirely sure how far to go with the incarnation. How human was Jesus? For a lot of them, the human side of Jesus is superficial.
>
> It's almost as though a lot of Christians think of Jesus as God

wearing a human mask. He's sort of faking it, pretending to be human. He pretends to perspire, his stomach only appears to gurgle because, of course, he's not really hungry. In fact, he doesn't really need to eat. So Jesus is the bionic Son of God who isn't really human. This is thought to be exalted Christology, but it's not. Orthodox Christology also embraces fully the humanity of Jesus.

What I'm saying is that the divine nature of Jesus should never militate against his full humanity. When that part gets lost, you end up with a pretty superficial understanding of Christology. For example, could Jesus read? 'Of course he could read! He's the Son of God!' That's not a good answer. At the age of three days, was Jesus fluent in Hebrew? Could he do quantum physics? Well, then, why does the book of Hebrews talk about him learning and so forth?

We find ourselves fussing and fuming over the divinity, but we miss his humanity. And from the historic point of view . . . that's just as serious an error as, say . . . to deny the divinity.[6]

Dr. Evans goes on to mention several things Christians miss about the humanity of Jesus when we fall into this kind of thinking:

Well, a big part of the atonement. He dies in our place as a human being who dies in our place. God didn't send an angel. And . . . there's the identification factor. We can identify with him: he was tempted as we are. How was he tempted if He was just God wearing a mask—faking it and pretending to be human? Again, that's Docetic Gnosticism—Jesus only appeared to be incarnate, only appeared to be human—and a lot of evangelical Christians come pretty close to that.

[And] . . . Jesus's own faith. . . . He tells his disciples to have faith. Jesus has a huge amount of credibility if we see him as fully human and he actually, as a human, has faith in God. Otherwise, well, that's easy for him to say! Good grief—he's been in heaven, and now he's walking around telling me to have faith?[7]

When we overlook or deny the human traits and characteristics of Jesus, we ignore what compels me more than anything else to love and appreciate the God who reveals himself in the person of Jesus: the fact that *God chose to come to us like this.*

If the man Jesus had been all-knowing and all-powerful like he was as the pre-incarnate Son, *before* becoming flesh, then what might appear to be great heroism, bravery, or self-sacrifice on his part would've actually been more like Superman rescuing someone from a burning building: it looks noble, worthy, and courageous, but in truth he was never in any real danger, and therefore he risked nothing.

If Jesus had known everything, then it would have been impossible to catch him off-guard or surprise him. If he were all-powerful, then nothing could have hurt him.

But I ask you: what courage would Jesus need if he were invincible to all the pain, suffering, loneliness, fear, and worry that you and I feel every day?

What honor would he deserve if he wasn't willing to suffer or endure anything to reach and save us?

And how unfair of him would it be to expect us to *follow him* if he had so many advantages that we simply don't have?

It would be like Superman asking us to follow him and fly like he does, but without giving us any superpowers. It's an impossible and ridiculous expectation. Further, why should we be expected to endure personal suffering, pain, or sacrifice for him if he wasn't really willing to do the same for us?

On the other hand, if Jesus was a real human being, then we can see just how low God was willing to stoop, humble himself, and suffer for us; and we can trust Jesus when he calls us to follow him, because we know he's walked in our shoes and knows what it's like to be human like we are.

During this book, we'll lay the scriptural foundations for the humanity of Jesus. In the process, we'll come face to face with a stunning, often shocking, picture of a God who is so passionately in love with us that he is willing to do, endure, and suffer just about *anything* to break through to us.

My hope is that we'll commit ourselves to serve the God who suffered, gave, and endured so much to reach, serve, and save us.

If it's true he did so much, then how will you respond?

What changes will you make to the way you live?

2

EMPTIED OUT

It's the 1992 Barcelona Olympics and the world is watching one of the greatest moments in sports history. British sprinter Derek Redmund is favored to win a gold medal in the 400 meters, but he tears his hamstring and collapses to the ground a third of the way through his race.

The runners leave him behind as he winces in pain, weeps, and tries to hide his tears. He realizes that his whole life's dedication, training, and dreams are gone.

Done.

Disbelief sets in. He looks around trying to decide what to do. Race officials run to him to help him up, but he shrugs them off, stands up on his own, and hobbles slowly like a crippled man around the track.

Crying.

Devastated.

As the crowd realizes Derek is trying to finish the race, they all rise to their feet to cheer him on.

The race is over. The other racers have left the track.

But he keeps hobbling.

Wincing.

Hurting.

Confused.

Agonized.

At the point of collapse.

Then, as he is rounding the final turn of the race, an older man runs down from the crowd, onto the track and out towards Derek. Security tries to stop him at first, but he says something to them and they let him pass onto the track.

The man approaches Derek from behind, so Derek doesn't see him, but when the man catches up to Derek, he puts his arm around him and hugs him. Derek bursts into tears of frustration, pain, agony, and disbelief, and buries his head in his father's embrace.

Derek's father tells his son that he doesn't have to do this, but Derek replies to him that, *yes, he does.*

And so they walk the final hundred meters together.

Father and son.

Arm in arm.

Derek's father provides the strength to get Derek over the finish line.

Derek finishes dead last, but he finishes.

Because of the help and support of his dad.

I love this story because, according to Paul's words in Philippians 2:5-11, it's a real-life parallel of what Jesus has done for us. In the race of our lives, things inevitably fall apart and we find ourselves broken, hurting, and at times barely able to go on.

And it's in these difficult times that Jesus comes down and meets us in the midst of our own brokenness, saying: *It's okay, I've got you. I'll carry you. I'll be your strength. Lean on me.*

Jesus fulfills the role for us that Derek's dad filled for Derek. And in Paul's letter to the Philippian Christians of the 1ˢᵗ century A.D., he urges them to live in unity and develop the mind and attitude of Christ Jesus, which he then describes with these amazing words:

> [5] Let the same mind be in you that was in Christ Jesus, [6] who, though he was in the form of God, did not regard equality with God as something to be exploited, [7] but emptied himself, taking the form of a slave, being born in human likeness.
>
> And being found in human form, [8] he humbled himself and became obedient to the point of death—even death on a cross.
>
> [9] Therefore God also highly exalted him and gave him the name that is above every name, [10] so that at the name of Jesus every knee should bend, in heaven and on earth and under the earth, [11] and every tongue should confess that Jesus Christ is Lord, to the glory of God the Father.[8]

A few things stand out to me about this: Paul says in verse 6 that while Jesus existed in the form of God, he didn't value his status or position ("*equality with God*") so much that he wasn't willing to let them go.

What does Paul mean by that? He means that, since Jesus existed as God long before he ever came to us in the person of Jesus, he would have been totally justified if he wanted to remain God in that exalted state with all his glory, majesty, authority, rank, and power.

But, amazingly, he was willing to let them go so he could stoop down to our level, meet us where we are, and save those of us who follow him. And that's precisely what Paul says Jesus did.

For me, the most shocking and surprising thing comes in

verses 7–8, when Paul says Jesus *"emptied himself . . . humbled himself."*

This was no accident.

No fluke.

Jesus chose to empty and humble himself.

On purpose.

As an act of the will.

Pre-meditated.

To the point of death.

What does it mean to say Jesus *"emptied himself?"* There are lots of possibilities, but the view I hold is that he emptied himself not of his divinity, but of his divine glory, majesty, and exalted status, including even his divine power and knowledge.

This is why I have no problem saying the man Jesus was not all-knowing or all-powerful (however you define those), and the writers of the New Testament clearly felt the same.

The Almighty God chose to become a vulnerable, weak, fully-dependent newborn who didn't even know how to walk, talk, or do basic addition or subtraction!

Now, why on earth would Jesus have chosen to do this?

Love.

A love for humanity that's so intense it's shocking and scary. What else but intense love could motivate someone to willingly set aside endless amounts of glory, majesty, honor, exaltation, power, knowledge, and authority in order to empty himself and endure rejection, loneliness, shame, insults, attacks, betrayal, weakness, fear, suffering, beatings, torture, and execution?

And if he was willing to go to such lengths for you and I, how else could we possibly respond but by thanking him, admiring him, loving him, and serving him? How else could we respond but by giving our lives back to the one died in our place to set us free?

Now, when I feel prideful or above doing certain things, I try to remember that if anyone had the right not to humble himself, it was Jesus; but he laid down that right. So if I claim to be a *follower (disciple) of Jesus*, then how could I not be willing to empty and humble myself on behalf of this broken world, like he did?

Because if I claim to be a follower of Jesus, but I don't actually follow Jesus, then I'm just a hypocrite.

How might God be calling you to empty and humble yourself to serve this hurting and broken world?

How might he be calling you to follow the example of Derek's dad, who left his comfortable and posh stadium seats in order to lower himself down to the level of his son who was broken, hurting, and in need of help?

What stops you from doing that right now with the people in your world?

3

A SHADY BIRTH

I was born into a loving family who eagerly planned for my arrival; unfortunately, far too many people don't have that experience. Many children are born to parents who weren't planning on having children, at least not at the time when they became pregnant; and some of those children feel like they weren't wanted, accepted, planned for, or loved by some members of their families.

Amazingly, I think Jesus knows exactly how they feel.

Each Christmas, the cute Nativity scene of Jesus's birth fills us with warm fuzzy feelings of love and bliss, but because of this we completely overlook how scandalous, shady, humiliating, and shameful his birth really was. We don't realize that the self-humbling and self-emptying of Jesus began before he was even born.[9]

Luke began the birth-story by mentioning three key details. God sent the angel Gabriel to a virgin engaged to be married, in order to tell her the Holy Spirit will come upon her, and that she will soon be pregnant as a result. So she is: 1) a virgin; 2) pledged

to be married; and 3) soon to be pregnant by God's Spirit! Here
are the words from Luke's gospel:

> [26] *In the sixth month the angel Gabriel was sent by God to a town in*
> *Galilee called Nazareth,* [27] *to a virgin engaged to a man whose name*
> *was Joseph, of the house of David. The virgin's name was Mary.* [28]
> *And he came to her and said, "Greetings, favored one! The Lord is*
> *with you."* [29]*But she was much perplexed by his words and pondered*
> *what sort of greeting this might be.* [30] *The angel said to her, "Do not*
> *be afraid, Mary, for you have found favor with God.* [31] *And now, you*
> *will conceive in your womb and bear a son, and you will name him*
> *Jesus.* [32] *He will be great, and will be called the Son of the Most High,*
> *and the Lord God will give to him the throne of his ancestor David.*
> [33]*He will reign over the house of Jacob forever, and of his kingdom*
> *there will be no end."* [34] *Mary said to the angel, "How can this be,*
> *since I am a virgin?"* [35] *The angel said to her, "The Holy Spirit will*
> *come upon you, and the power of the Most High will overshadow*
> *you; therefore the child to be born will be holy; he will be called Son of*
> *God.*[10]

When an ancient Jewish couple wanted to marry, they made a
formal pledge of marriage and then had one year to prepare
themselves while still living with their parents. During that year,
the couple was considered legally married, but they would not
live together or have sexual relations until the actual wedding.

We must also remember that God and his people took sexual
purity very seriously, and adultery was so offensive that Jewish
law called for adulterers to be stoned to death.[11]

In fact, because couples like Joseph and Mary, who were
pledged to be married but not yet fully married, were legally
considered husband and wife, Mary's pregnancy while pledged to

Joseph would have been interpreted by their families and society as adultery. According to Jewish law, Joseph could have had her executed.

In fact, Mary's pregnancy was so scandalous that, at first, even Joseph did not believe her. He was going to divorce her, presumably to avoid the shame and humiliation of staying together.[12]

He only believed her later because an angel appeared to him explaining everything, but their parents, families, friends, and neighbors never received any angelic explanations and must have viewed them with suspicion, shame, rejection, and disgust.

When it comes time for Jesus's actual birth, we again see these themes of rejection, shame, and disgust, which most Christians completely overlook. Here are the words from the next chapter in Luke's gospel:

> [1] *In those days a decree went out from Emperor Augustus that all the world should be registered.* [2] *This was the first registration and was taken while Quirinius was governor of Syria.* [3] *All went to their own towns to be registered.* [4] *Joseph also went from the town of Nazareth in Galilee to Judea, to the city of David called Bethlehem, because he was descended from the house and family of David.* [5] *He went to be registered with Mary, to whom he was engaged and who was expecting a child.* [6] *While they were there, the time came for her to deliver her child.* [7] *And she gave birth to her firstborn son and wrapped him in bands of cloth, and laid him in a manger, because there was no place for them in the inn.*[13]

In verse 3, Joseph and Mary go to Joseph's own town to register for the census; and since he came from the family of David, they go to Bethlehem. Now, it's almost certain that Joseph had tons of (extended) family living in, or staying in, Bethlehem during the census, because they all had to go there to be counted. His whole extended family would have been in Bethlehem at that time, because that was the hometown of his whole family's lineage.

This is very important, because verse 5 says Joseph went '*with Mary, to whom he was engaged and who was expecting a child.*" Again, they were engaged and pledged to be married, but they weren't yet legally married, which means according to Jewish law, they should not be sexually active or pregnant.

Joseph's family would have assumed that either Mary and Joseph had pre-marital sex or Mary committed adultery, both of which were completely scandalous and shameful for their whole family.

Verse 7 says Mary wrapped Jesus in cloths and placed him in a manger, because there was no room for them in the inn. Most people today think of a manger as part of our warm fuzzy Christmas stories, but in that context, everyone knew mangers were used as feeding troughs to feed animals. They were not nice or glamorous, and no one would have wanted to lay their newborn baby in one. They were filthy.

And having to go to an inn implies that, in a town overflowing with Joseph's whole extended family, Joseph and Mary were forced to go to an inn because they were not welcome in the homes of the extended family of Joseph.

But that word translated *inn* can also refer to the upper room of a Jewish house, which would imply Joseph and Mary knocked on his family's doors and asked to come in, but were told the rooms were full and were then shut out to fend for themselves.

Now even if the upper rooms were full of Joseph's relatives, you would think they would have seen his desperate situation and made room for them in their homes by giving them the upper room.

But they didn't.

So we must ask ourselves: why on earth would Joseph and Mary be forced to give birth alone and outside, placing Jesus in a feeding trough for animals, when Joseph would have had a huge extended family living and staying in houses all over Bethlehem?

What could possibly explain why Joseph's family shut them out?

I think the answer is simple: Joseph, Mary, and Jesus were not welcome.

They weren't wanted or accepted.

Joseph's family saw this pregnancy as so shameful, unacceptable, and embarrassing that they rejected Joseph, Mary, and their illegitimate child.

They thought Joseph, Mary, and Jesus were bringing so much shame and embarrassment onto the whole family that they wouldn't even let them in their homes.

But how disgusted would they need to be in order to reject their own family when they were on the verge of giving birth?

And why on earth would the God of the universe choose such scandalous and shameful circumstances to come to us?

He could have come to us as anyone, so why not come as Caesar, who was the most powerful man at that time? Why not come as some exalted and mighty king, ruler, or warrior to show everyone just how strong and powerful he is?

Why would God, the creator of the cosmos and everything in it, choose to come to us as a weak, rejected, illegitimate child of so much shame, embarrassment, and scorn?

Maybe it's so we could know just how much he cares for and

identifies with the most unwanted, rejected, and broken people around.

Maybe it's so Jesus can look at all the rejected and unwanted children of our world and say to them: *me too.*

After all, Jesus knows exactly how they feel.

The humanity of Jesus reveals the ultimate paradox: the *humble* God. Before Jesus, being *humble* was not a compliment; it was an insult describing the weak and powerless. But Jesus's birth demands this paradox. The creator of the universe arrived on the scene despised and rejected by most of his family.

In Jesus, the creator of the universe made himself approachable to humanity. This is why Paul said Jesus is *"the image of the invisible God;"* and that in him, *"the whole fullness of deity dwells bodily."*[4] Paul was saying that when we look at Jesus, we see God!

What could have possibly caused God to do something so crazy and radical?

Love.

And if this story is true, then how does that change the way we view God? How might it affect the way we view those who are weak, helpless, oppressed, or cast aside by the power players in our society?

When I think of Jesus willingly coming to us in this way, it leaves me in awe.

What a breathtaking demonstration of love!

The question is: how will we respond?

4

HUMAN LIMITATIONS

Christian theology has always said Jesus is both fully divine and fully human, but if that's true, then how is it possible? There are two main views of how this is true, and we're going to explore them in this chapter.

The Two Views of Jesus's Humanity

The first view, which I will refer to as the *superhuman view*, is believed by most Christians today who don't think deeply about these issues. This view assumes that since God is all-knowing and all-powerful (however you define those), Jesus must therefore be all-knowing and all-powerful, too. Otherwise, they think, he couldn't be divine.

The people who take this view ignore, overlook, or explain away verses that clearly show Jesus in very human terms as not all-powerful or all-knowing. For these people, those kinds of verses threaten their understanding of the divinity of Jesus, so they largely ignore them and hope no one notices.

The second view is called the *kenotic view*, because it is based on the Greek word Paul uses in Philippians 2:5–11, when he talks about how Jesus willingly *emptied himself.* The Greek word Paul uses to refer to Jesus emptying himself is *kenosis.* Here is that section of scripture again, so we're all sure what Paul is talking about:

> [5] *Let the same mind be in you that was in Christ Jesus,* [6] *who, though he was in the form of God, did not regard equality with God as something to be exploited,* [7]*but emptied himself, taking the form of a slave, being born in human likeness. And being found in human form,* [8] *he humbled himself and became obedient to the point of death— even death on a cross.*
>
> [9] *Therefore God also highly exalted him and gave him the name that is above every name,* [10] *so that at the name of Jesus every knee should bend, in heaven and on earth and under the earth,* [11]*and every tongue should confess that Jesus Christ is Lord, to the glory of God the Father.*[15]

This view is very different, because it says Jesus *emptied himself* when he became a human being, which means he would have emptied himself of his divine form, glory, knowledge (omniscience), power (omnipotence), and anything else he needed to leave behind to become a real human being just like you and I.

To put that into perspective, think about this: it is like someone risking their own pain, suffering, mutilation, and death to save you and me from a burning building. This is what Jesus did to rescue us from our own death and destruction.

But is there evidence for this view in the gospels? We will spend the rest of this chapter unpacking the instances where Jesus's human limitations are obvious and undeniable, so we can have no doubt how far God was willing to go, and how low he was willing to stoop, to rescue and save us.

What Jesus Knows

In this section, we're going to start by examining obvious incidents where Jesus doesn't know everything.

Let's first look at Luke 2:52, which says Jesus *"increased in wisdom and in years."* [16] How can someone who knows everything increase in wisdom? That's impossible.

Jesus was a normal child who had to learn how to walk, talk, and eat just like everyone else. Jesus wasn't born knowing everything, which will be made even clearer in the rest of this chapter.

The second place we're going to look is Mark 5:24–34, where a bleeding woman touches Jesus's cloak as he is on the way to heal someone else. Jesus feels healing power go out of him, the woman is healed, and then he turns around and asks, *"who touched my clothes?"* Here is the whole interaction:

> [24] And a large crowd followed him and pressed in on him. [25] Now there was a woman who had been suffering from hemorrhages for twelve years. [26] She had endured much under many physicians, and had spent all that she had; and she was no better, but rather grew worse. [27] She had heard about Jesus, and came up behind him in the crowd and touched his cloak, [28] for she said, "If I but touch his clothes, I will be made well." [29] Immediately her hemorrhage stopped; and she felt in her body that she was healed of her disease. [30] Immediately aware that power had gone forth from him, Jesus turned about in the crowd and said, "Who touched my clothes?" [31] And his disciples said to him, "You see the crowd pressing in on you; how can you say, 'Who touched me?' [32] He looked all around to see who had done it. [33] But the

woman, knowing what had happened to her, came in fear and
trembling, fell down before him, and told him the whole truth. *[34]He*
said to her, "Daughter, your faith has made you well; go in peace, and
be healed of your disease."[7]

The people who hold the first view of Christ's humanity, who
believe he is omnipotent and omniscient, try to explain this away
by saying Jesus's question was rhetorical, and that he actually
knew the answer the whole time. But nothing in this scene
sounds rhetorical. Jesus is surrounded by lots of people as he was
walking to someone else, then someone touches him as his back
is to the crowd, and then he turns around and asks who touched
him.

That doesn't sound rhetorical at all to me. It sounds like Jesus
asked because he honestly didn't know, just like you and I do
every day.

The third place we're going to look is in Mark 13:32, when
Jesus says he doesn't know the time of his own return! Here are
the words from Mark's gospel:

But about that day or hour no one knows, neither the angels in
heaven, nor the Son, but only the Father. Beware, keep alert; for you
do not know when the time will come.[18]

What?

How can Jesus not know the time of his own return?

Are you kidding, Jesus?

While it seems pretty incomprehensible to me that Jesus
doesn't know the time of his own return, I didn't make that up.

Jesus said it.

Not me.

The people who hold the superhuman view have no way of explaining this. Some of them think Jesus was only pretending not to know. But if Jesus is pretending not to know when he really does, then he is lying; and now you have a much bigger theological problem to deal with.

The second view, the kenotic view, has no problem with this whatsoever, because this shows us just how far and low Jesus was willing to empty himself when he became human.

The fourth place we're going to look is Mark 14:32–36, where Jesus asks his Father to take his cup (or destiny) of suffering from him, if there is another way to save the human race he was sent to save. Here is the whole passage so you can see it:

> 32 They went to a place called Gethsemane; and he said to his disciples, "Sit here while I pray." 33 He took with him Peter and James and John, and began to be distressed and agitated. 34 And he said to them, "I am deeply grieved, even to death; remain here, and keep awake." 35 And going a little farther, he threw himself on the ground and prayed that, if it were possible, the hour might pass from him. 36 He said, "Abba, Father, for you all things are possible; remove this cup from me; yet, not what I want, but what you want."19

In verse 35, Jesus prays that, if possible, the hour might pass from him. This means Jesus doesn't know if it's possible or not, so he's asking his Father. He's saying that, if it is possible to not drink this cup of suffering, and still save the world he came to save, then that's what he wants.

But if it's not possible, then he's willing to deny what he wants to do, and instead do what his father wants him to do. But if Jesus doesn't know what is possible and what's not possible, as this passage clearly shows, then obviously there are things he doesn't know.

The fifth place we're going to look is Hebrews 5:8, which says Jesus *"learned obedience."*[20] This is a very significant statement, because how can Jesus learn anything if he already knows everything? The only way this verse makes any sense is if we assume there were things Jesus didn't know that he learned later in life, like obedience.

These verses present all kinds of headaches and problems for the Christians who subscribe to the all-powerful, all-knowing view of Jesus's humanity. They view all these verses as threats to the divinity of Jesus, so they try to cover them up and interpret them in ways that do not match the context of the verses themselves.

On the other hand, if we take the kenotic view of Jesus, then the fact that he emptied himself of things like his divine knowledge and power does not contradict or threaten his divine status. Instead, these show us just how low Jesus was willing to empty and humble himself in order to reach and save us.

In fact, that's why these kinds of verses leave me in awe.

The Limits of Jesus's Power

There are even verses that demonstrate Jesus's limited power. But for those who take the kenotic view from Paul's words in Philippians 2:5–11, these human limitations don't threaten the divinity of Jesus. Rather, they show us just how far he emptied and humbled himself when he became human.

The passage we're looking at is Mark 6:1–6, when Jesus is rejected in his hometown of Nazareth. Here are the words from Mark's gospel:

¹ He left that place and came to his hometown, and his disciples followed him. ² On the sabbath he began to teach in the synagogue, and many who heard him were astounded. They said, "Where did this man get all this? What is this wisdom that has been given to him? What deeds of power are being done by his hands! ³ Is not this the carpenter, the son of Mary and brother of James and Joses and Judas and Simon, and are not his sisters here with us?" And they took offense at him. ⁴ Then Jesus said to them, "Prophets are not without honor, except in their hometown, and among their own kin, and in their own house." ⁵ And he could do no deed of power there, except that he laid his hands on a few sick people and cured them. ⁶ And he was amazed at their unbelief."[21]

This is absolutely stunning!

Verses 5–6 say Jesus couldn't do any deeds of power except heal a few sick people by laying hands on them and curing them. His power was limited because of the lack of faith of the people in his hometown.

Notice: it doesn't say Jesus didn't do any deeds of power; it says he couldn't do any.

Why?

Because of the unbelief of the people.

The power of Jesus was not his own. It didn't come from him. The power of Jesus was really the power of God working through him, and that power was dependent on the faith of the people; and since the people apparently had no faith, he couldn't do any deeds of power there. This is stunning and certainly not the description of an all-powerful being who can do whatever he wants, whenever he wants.

The first view, which I called the superhuman view, has no way to explain away this fact, so they try to ignore it and hope no one notices. In the second view, the kenotic view, this doesn't hinder or diminish the divinity of Jesus at all, because we recognize this as Jesus emptying himself of his divine power (his omnipotence) before he became human.

The human limitations of Jesus show us that he wasn't like a superhero who was invincible. Instead, he was a human being just like you and me, with human limitations, realities, and hindrances. That also means we can look to him as the model for how the rest of us can live our lives.

How do we respond to someone who emptied himself of so many things to reach and save us?

When I think about how much Jesus emptied and humbled himself of things like his divine knowledge and power, it makes me want to lay down my life for him.

It makes me want to live my life completely for him.

How will you respond?

5

TEMPTATIONS

If you ever tried to convince me to do something I didn't want to do by offering me black licorice, you would fail every time. Why? Because I hate black licorice! But if you offered me *carne asada* burritos, which I love, then I might actually do whatever it was you wanted me to do.

What do black licorice and burritos have to do with the temptation of Jesus?

They show us that we can only be tempted by that which we find desirable or pleasing in some way, but that doesn't mean those desires are necessarily bad. Unfortunately, it seems like most Christians misunderstand temptation, believing it to be inherently sinful, and insist that if we were only more holy (like Jesus), then we would not feel so tempted.

They view Jesus as so perfect, holy, and divine that it was literally impossible for him to sin, and therefore impossible for him to have been tempted. But as we will see below, this contradicts scripture and distorts the biblical view of Jesus. Hebrews 2:14–18 says this about Jesus:

[14] Since, therefore, the children share flesh and blood, he himself likewise shared the same things, so that through death he might destroy the one who has the power of death, that is, the devil, [15] and free those who all their lives were held in slavery by the fear of death. [16] For it is clear that he did not come to help angels, but the descendants of Abraham. [17] Therefore he had to become like his brothers and sisters in every respect, so that he might be a merciful and faithful high priest in the service of God, to make a sacrifice of atonement for the sins of the people. [18] Because he himself was tested [tempted] by what he suffered, he is able to help those who are being tested [tempted].[22]

Two things stand out to me about this: 1) Jesus had to share in our humanity *"in every respect"* in order to free us from our own sin and death; 2) He can only help us through our own temptations and tests, *"Because he himself was tested* [tempted] *by what he suffered."*[23] So Jesus had to suffer being tempted and tested, like us in every way, otherwise he would not be able to save or help us when we are tempted and tested.

This chapter will look at three instances where Jesus was tempted, and discover what his responses say about his humanity.

Hunger

In Luke 4:1–13, we first see Jesus being tempted by Satan. Here is the account:

[1] Jesus, full of the Holy Spirit, returned from the Jordan and was led by the Spirit in the wilderness, [2] where for forty days he was tempted by the devil. He ate nothing at all during those days, and when they

*were over, he was famished. ³ The devil said to him, "If you are the
Son of God, command this stone to become a loaf of bread." ⁴ Jesus
answered him, "It is written, 'One does not live by bread alone.'"*

*⁵ Then the devil led him up and showed him in an instant all the
kingdoms of the world. ⁶ And the devil said to him, "To you I will give
their glory and all this authority; for it has been given over to me, and
I give it to anyone I please. ⁷ If you, then, will worship me, it will all
be yours." ⁸ Jesus answered him, "It is written, 'Worship the Lord your
God, and serve only him.'"*

*⁹ Then the devil took him to Jerusalem, and placed him on the
pinnacle of the temple, saying to him, "If you are the Son of God,
throw yourself down from here, ¹⁰ for it is written, 'He will command
his angels concerning you, to protect you,' ¹¹ and 'On their hands they
will bear you up, so that you will not dash your foot against a stone.'"
¹² Jesus answered him, "It is said, 'Do not put the Lord your God to the
test.'" ¹³ When the devil had finished every test, he departed from him
until an opportune time.*²⁴

In Luke 4:1–2, it says Jesus was tempted for 40 days, during
which he did not eat, and that he was hungry afterwards. I find it
fascinating that Satan can exploit something as neutral and ordinary as hunger for his purposes.

Hunger isn't bad.

It just happens to be what Jesus felt at that moment, so Satan
started there.

It would be much easier to notice and resist Satan if he really
did have big horns, carry a pitchfork, and wear red tights like our
popular images portray him. Unfortunately, he usually uses the
subtlest means available. For Jesus, it was simple hunger.

In fact, the subtle and conniving nature of Satan makes me
think of the classic line from the movie *The Usual Suspects*: "The

greatest trick the devil ever pulled was convincing the world he didn't exist." Unfortunately, our enemy is very astute, and we should never underestimate him.

The first temptation Satan hits Jesus with is, "*If you are the Son of God, command this stone to become a loaf of bread.*"[25] Satan knows Jesus is hungry, so he tempts him with the seemingly harmless act of feeding himself.

But this temptation hides a deeper struggle: Will Jesus use his authority and power as the Son of God to satisfy his own desires, or will he use them to satisfy God's desires?

Jesus responds by quoting part of Deuteronomy 8:3 to Satan: "*It is written: 'one does not live by bread alone'.*"[26] The rest of that verse reads: "*. . . but by every word that comes from the mouth of the Lord.*"[27]

Notice: Jesus is the *Son of God,* but he doesn't battle Satan with all-out cosmic warfare. Instead he uses the very human method of grounding his identity, purpose, and calling in God's word. Jesus battles Satan as an authentic human being. His response shows that he will remain faithful to God's word alone.

All the Kingdoms

In another temptation, Satan offers Jesus authority over all the kingdoms of the world if he will only bow down and worship Satan.[28] This is an intriguing offer because Jesus knows he is God's promised *messiah*, the king who will one day rule over Israel and all the nations of the earth.[29]

That is Jesus's whole destiny and purpose.

So Satan offers Jesus what Jesus knows will one day be his, but there is a catch: Jesus must switch his allegiance from his father to Satan.

If he is willing to do that, then he can have his destiny to rule over the nations in an instant.

Think about the offer Satan gives him. Jesus wouldn't need to go through any pain or suffering like he would if he chooses his father's way. He wouldn't need to endure any more shame, or even the cross. Satan offers Jesus the easy way to attain the power and authority that was rightfully his—if he'll just switch his allegiance.

This, by the way, is the exact offer the Emperor makes to Anakin Skywalker in *Star Wars*. Anakin wants to fulfill his destiny and be the most powerful Jedi he can be, but he doesn't want to take the slow road of learning as a disciple, an apprentice, of Yoda. So when the emperor offers Anakin his destiny of being the most powerful Jedi now if he will just switch his allegiance from Yoda to the Emperor, Anakin takes the offer.

But where Anakin takes the bait and switches his allegiance to the Dark Side, Jesus remains faithful by again grounding his identity, destiny, and purpose in God's word alone: *"It is written: 'Worship the Lord your God, and serve him only'."*[30]

Jesus's faithfulness to his father's will amazes me, because judging by how much he suffers in the gospels, the thought of instant power and authority without any pain or suffering must have seemed pretty enticing.

The Temple

In the third temptation, Satan challenged Jesus to test God by throwing himself off the temple to see if God would send his angels to catch him.[31] Jesus responded with scripture again, this time Deuteronomy 6:16: *"It says, 'Do not put the Lord your God to the test'."*[32]

Jesus could have taken up Satan's challenge, but that would have meant entering into Satan's twisted world on Satan's own terms, which Jesus refused to do. We demonstrate great ignorance when we knowingly step into Satan's world, and then demand that God rescue us once we realize we were wrong.

Knowing Jesus shared in our humanity in every way, and that he was tempted like we are makes me appreciate him so much more than if he had not done that. It shows us that he really was willing to empty and humble himself down into the trenches of our human condition to rescue us. And because he was tested and tempted but did not sin, we can trust him to help guide us through our own tests and temptations.[33]

How does this affect us? In a few ways. To begin with, I think far too many Christians beat themselves up spiritually because they believe temptation itself is wrong; and because they often feel tempted, they think they are hopelessly sinful or messed up.

But that can't be true because, as we just saw, scripture says Jesus was tempted yet he did not sin; so it's not temptation which determines whether we sin or not, but how we respond to temptation. And since Jesus was fully human and like us in every way, we can all follow his basic method to conquer our own temptations.

We can all ground our identity, worth, and calling in God's word, which is exactly what Jesus did here.

How might you emulate Jesus the next time you are tempted or tested?

How might you ground your identity, destiny, and purpose in God's word alone?

6

THE POWER OF TOUCH

Let's stop and think about what kinds of people are the most excluded, abandoned, condemned, and marginalized in our culture. Think about how our country treats people like child molesters, terrorists, felons, illegal immigrants, victims of HIV/AIDS, or even members of the LGBTQ community. They're mistreated time and time again.

In Jesus's day, no one suffered more than lepers and people with other similar skin diseases. In this chapter, let's see how Jesus interacted with a leper so we can see his beautiful and awesome humanity on display again:

> [12] Once, when he was in one of the cities, there was a man covered with leprosy. When he saw Jesus, he bowed with his face to the ground and begged him, "Lord, if you choose, you can make me clean." [13] Then Jesus stretched out his hand, touched him, and said, "I do choose. Be made clean." Immediately the leprosy left him. [14] And he ordered him to tell no one. "Go," he said, "and show yourself to the priest, and, as Moses commanded, make an offering for your cleansing, for a testimony to

them." ¹⁵ But now more than ever the word about Jesus spread abroad;
many crowds would gather to hear him and to be cured of their
diseases. ¹⁶ But he would withdraw to deserted places and pray.³⁴

In verse 12, it says there was a man covered with leprosy who
bows down so his face is to the ground, and then says Jesus can
make him clean if he wants to.

First: we need to say a few things about the leprosy this man
has. The Greek word is *lepra,* which can refer to leprosy or a
number of similar skin conditions; but they all carry lots of physical disfigurement, pain, and discomfort. Not only that, but the
disease carries lots of social pain and stigma, too.

Second: it's interesting that the leper didn't ask Jesus to heal
him. He asked him to make him clean. But why would he do that?
Why not ask Jesus to be healed?

The reason he asks this is because the primary concern for
Jews in the time of Jesus was to be *ceremonially clean,* as opposed
to being *ceremonially unclean.* What do these terms mean? Let's
take a look.

God gave Israel a system of ceremonial cleanliness that was
supposed to be a picture of God's holiness. That meant that to go
before a holy God in his temple, Jews during that time needed to
prepare themselves and avoid certain things that would make
them ceremonially unclean. It was a way for God to teach Israel
about his holiness, so they would learn to take it seriously.

There were many ways a Jew could be made ceremonially
unclean, and the ceremonially unclean people would need to
cleanse themselves to be made ceremonially clean. But God
always gave the ceremonially unclean people ways to purify
themselves and become ceremonially clean.

But by the days of Jesus, the Jewish religious leaders started neglecting the *ceremonial* status, and started viewing *people* as clean or unclean. The unclean people were viewed as permanently and hopelessly unclean and unfit. These people were viewed by others as cursed and rejected by God, so they were shown almost no pity or compassion.

In fact, they were viewed very similarly to India's class of untouchables that make up the bottom of the social order. People in India don't help the untouchables because Indians are Hindus, which means they believe in karma and reincarnation. Because of this, they think the untouchables are getting what they deserve, so they don't want to interfere with karma or fate by helping them.

Lepers were viewed in the day of Jesus just like the untouchables are in India. Lepers were viewed by the Jewish religious leaders not as being *ceremonially unclean*, but as being *unclean people* who had no hope of being made *clean* ever again. They were marginalized, ostracized, and completely rejected from normal Jewish society.

That also meant that, according to these traditions, anyone who touched a leper would be made *unclean* as well. For rabbis, touching a leper was like touching a corpse, because the lepers were counted as a sort of living-dead status.

Because of this, lepers were cut off completely from Jewish society: they lived in their own leper towns, and were unable to see their family or kids during celebrations like weddings, birthdays, or synagogue.

They had to shout: "*Unclean! Unclean!*" whenever they came within 100 meters of other clean Jews. Everyone avoided them, and there was almost no compassion for these people because most Jews thought they were getting paid back for some hidden sin by either them or their parents.

Most Jews thought God was giving the lepers exactly what they deserved, which meant Jews had almost no desire to help them, alleviate their pain, or rescue them from their situations.

Our Uncleanliness

The leper Jesus encountered fell down with his face to the ground and said Jesus could make him clean if he wanted to. We can almost hear and sense the desperation in this man's words: he was the victim of a brutal system of abandonment, scorn, and isolation, but he knew Jesus could end that and make him *clean*.

I absolutely love the compassion of Jesus's response:

He reached out his hand and *touched* this unclean leper. Then he made him *clean*, and the leprosy left him.[35]

This is why I love Jesus.

Jesus could have simply healed this man without touching him, but he didn't.

He touched him because he knew the man needed it.

Jesus touched the *untouchable.*

Can you imagine what that touch must have felt like for that man? That was probably the first time any healthy person had touched him in years. Can you imagine the tears of joy and relief that must have overwhelmed him when Jesus touched him, made him clean, and healed him from his leprosy?

Studies have shown how much love and affection are communicated through physical touch.

We crave it.

We need it.

And we'll do almost anything to get it.

THE POWER OF TOUCH   41

We normally get this touch through parents, family members, children, neighbors, co-workers, friends, spouses, and lots of other people, but imagine being shut off completely from the touch and company of these people, because you had leprosy and couldn't go near them.

This disease, and others like it, eats away at the flesh so the flesh looks like it's rotting away and dying. People were repulsed.

Imagine having no one shake your hand, hug you, or kiss you for years.

This was the reality lepers lived through in the time of Jesus, which makes the touch of Jesus so incredibly powerful.

There is another thing I want to highlight about this text: when Jesus touched the unclean leper, Jesus should have been made unclean, but the opposite happened. When Jesus touched the man, Jesus's cleanliness made the man clean.

The Jewish religious system during the time of Jesus taught that people needed to be clean before they could approach God.

But Jesus reversed that.

Jesus demonstrated and taught that you could approach God *as you are*, and he will make you clean later.

That means we don't need to try and clean ourselves up before we draw near to God; we just need to get ourselves to him and let him take care of the rest.

This is a true revolution of grace because it flipped every religion, and every religious system, on its head.

Just like that, Jesus destroyed every religion ever invented.

For example, when I was in my early twenties and still not a follower of Jesus, I remember talking with my dad about this very topic. I had partied hard since I was young, and all my friends and I did when we went out was go to bars and parties to get wasted.

I remember talking with my dad about how I wanted to go to church, but I felt that I couldn't because I always went to bars and parties with my friends. I remember telling my dad that I would never be a Christian because Christians don't go to bars.

My dad, who was much wiser than I ever gave him credit for, asked me simply: *Why not?*

And I had no answer to his question.

I said I didn't know why they don't go to bars, but they just don't. My dad told me that people criticized Jesus for being a drunkard, because he hung around with all the wrong people too.[36]

My dad, in his wisdom, was trying to correct my flawed thinking. I thought I needed to clean myself up before I drew near to Jesus by not drinking or going to bars with my friends; but my dad knew that I shouldn't worry about that, and that I should instead focus on getting myself to Jesus, so he could make me clean and take care of everything else.

In fact, I think this is one of the main roles of Christians: we're called to get ourselves and others to Jesus, so he can make us clean and deal with the rest of our life. Making people clean is his job, not ours. Unfortunately, too often Christians forget this and switch it back to how it was before Jesus came.

Too many Christians think it's our job to be the world's morality police, but they're wrong.

When we fall into that trap, we demand that people clean themselves up before coming to Jesus, God, or church.

But that's not the Gospel.

That's not the *good news* of Jesus.

The good news of Jesus says: *just come to me, and I'll make you clean!*

If this is true, then what can we say about how the humanity of Jesus is expressed in this story?

If we're really honest, I bet many of us feel like this leper. We feel alone, abandoned, rejected, forgotten, unwanted, excluded, and left out, and we need the touch of Jesus to heal us and make us clean.

Some of us have tried everything to try to fill the void in our hearts and lives, but nothing has been able to heal us or make us new. I tried to fill the void in my heart and life by partying. In fact, I lived that way for about 10 years until I was finally forced to realize that lifestyle left me more empty and unfulfilled than when I started.

Until I came to Jesus, nothing worked.

And some of us need to come to Jesus, too.

In fact, the very first time I ever went to the college group I came to faith in, as I walked in alone and not knowing anyone, the first person I saw was an acquaintance I had during my junior high and high school years. I was so relieved to see him, because that meant that at least I knew one person there and wasn't completely on my own.

But I'll never forget the first words out of that friend's mouth when he saw me there. He looked at me and did a double-take to make sure it was me.

Then he said: "Greg Haugh! You're the last person I expected to see here!"

And I told him: "I know, tell me about it."

We had known each other since we were in junior high. Although we were never close, he knew how much I had partied and how far I was from God during all those years. And when he said that to me in a sort of joking way, I smiled back and knew he was right.

I was the last person I was expecting to be there, too.

But there I was.

The life of partying failed to deliver the true joy, meaning, and purpose I thought it would give me.

And so, with nowhere else to turn, I went to the one place I hadn't tried: Jesus.

My life looked great on the outside, but inside I was an absolute wreck who desperately needed Jesus. I didn't know how badly I needed him until I started going to that college group. Once I discovered Jesus—or rather he discovered me—I was so transformed and changed, and the only thing I wanted to do with my life was tell more people about him.

I tell you this so you don't fall into the religious trap of trying to make ourselves clean, or good, before we come to Jesus, God, or church.

We can't.

Just come to him, and he'll make us new and clean.

Now I know that to be true, because that's what he did with me; and that's what he has done with countless young people I've worked with since coming to faith about 15 years ago.

Who Jesus Accepts

There are people everywhere in our world who need the touch of Jesus, literally and figuratively, and are waiting for us, his people, to provide it.

Jesus can't go into the slums and hug people, but we can.

Paul says we are *"ambassadors for Christ,"* which means we're the representatives of Jesus on earth, and we are called to go touch, heal, and love people in his name and authority.[37] This is especially true of the people who live on the fringes of society, like lepers and untouchables.

The Gospel, or good news, of Jesus is supposed to be incredibly great news for incredibly great sinners.

But too often we diminish it until it becomes okay news for fairly nice people.

The reason the good news of Jesus is great news is because it's for absolutely everyone.

No one is excluded.

No one is forgotten.

No one is marginalized.

No matter how sinful and evil they may be.

Think of someone you know personally, who you think is beyond the realm of coming to Jesus. Think of the worst, most unforgivable people you know. Because these are exactly the kinds of people the gospel is for.

I know because I used to be one of those people, and now I'm sitting here writing books about Jesus, trying to draw as many people to him as I can.

I'm proof that no one is beyond God's reach.

In fact, I helped start a church in Chile from 2010 to 2014, which we started to reach out to all the Chilean skateboarders, surfers, and athletes the churches there weren't reaching. And one of the ways we did this was playing soccer—which is hugely popular in Latin America—with the prisoners at the local prison to develop relationships with them and share with them about Jesus after we finished playing.

Most of the prisoners didn't want to hear about Jesus if that's all people wanted to do with them when they visited. Because of this, we started going in with a soccer team so we could play with the prisoners and have fun together. It would always open them up to us sharing our faith with them after.

After going in the first couple times, the prison started to ask us back to visit prisoners in other areas, because they loved the positive impact we were having on the prisoners. After a while, we were going twice every month and being sent to each and every section of the prison. The prisoners and administrators kept inviting us back for more, and we kept coming.

In fact, word got out to the administrators of other prisons, and then we were being invited there, too. We accepted, and God did so many amazing things through our work with those prisoners. All we did was use soccer to build bridges with the prisoners, get to know them, and then have them listen to our stories and words about Jesus after we played soccer with them.

In fact, many of the prisoners we were with had life sentences. These were murderers, rapists, molesters, criminals, thieves, and everyone else you can imagine. While we laughed with the prisoners and got to know them, we also realized that for many of them, they would never see the outside of that jail.

They were there for life.

And for these kinds of prisoners, Jesus is their only chance.

They know that in this life, they will never be free.

That was why we took this calling and ministry so seriously. We knew this ministry had eternal consequences for these prisoners, and they might not have anyone else ever share the gospel with them.

I can't tell you how powerful it is to watch a condemned murderer, rapist, or thief realize that even though they have blown it with this life they were given, they know they can be free in the life to come if they recognize Jesus as their Lord and savior.

I can't tell you how powerful and moving it is to watch these kinds of hardened criminals break down and weep like little chil-dren when they hear that Jesus can give them the one thing they'll never have in that jail on this side of eternity: freedom.

I tell you this so we don't forget that the good news of Jesus is actually incredible news for the biggest sinners in our society; we shouldn't diminish it into okay news for okay people.

My challenge for us as we finish this chapter is to ask God how he can use us to touch and move people with the incredible love and grace of Jesus.

And who knows? You might be the first and only person to ever tell them about Jesus.

Please don't take that lightly, because at the end of the day, that's the most important thing any of us can ever do.

7

TEARS OF COMPASSION

"Jesus began to weep."[38] One of the shortest verses in the Bible, yet the words overflow with emotion, wonder, insight, truth, and mystery.

I remember being stunned as a new believer when I first read about Jesus weeping, because like many people, I grew up thinking Jesus was basically the docile, boring, tame, monotone Jesus I saw on TV or in most Christmas programs. I also thought God was basically some cold, harsh, cosmic policeman who was just out to get everyone and make sure no one had any fun.

But if Jesus is *"the image of the invisible God,"* and the one in whom *"the whole fullness of deity dwells bodily,"*[39] as Paul says he is, then that means God reveals himself to us most clearly in the person of Jesus Christ.

This means that when we see Jesus, we see God.

And if that's true, then that also means the tears of Jesus reveal something very truthful and heartbreaking about the heart of God. If Jesus's heart breaks, which it clearly does in these scenes where he weeps, then that reveals to us how the heart of God breaks when he sees his children suffering or in pain.

That is a radically different picture of God than most of us heard growing up.

It's also one that many people are simply unprepared for. But I am now convinced that it's impossible for us to understand God, ourselves, or our own pain and suffering without reflecting deeply on the tears of Jesus and what they tell us about the heart of God.

Jesus weeps once in the Gospel of John and once in the Gospel of Luke; yet because his tears are so crucial for understanding the heart of God, we will address John's gospel here and save the story from Luke for next chapter.

The death and healing of Lazarus in John 11:1–44 is incredibly fascinating. I'm going to work through it here to make sure we're clear about what happens. Martha and Mary are sisters and friends of Jesus. In fact, it was Mary who anointed Jesus's feet and wiped them with her hair. Their brother Lazarus, who Jesus loves, has become ill, and they send a message to him so he can presumably come heal him. But when Jesus hears about the illness, he says this:

> [4]"This illness does not lead to death; rather it is for God's glory, so that the Son of God may be glorified through it." . . . [6] after having heard that Lazarus was ill, he stayed two days longer. . . .
>
> [11]He told them, ". . . Lazarus has fallen asleep, but I am going there to awaken him." [12] The disciples said to him, "Lord, if he has fallen asleep, he will be all right." [13] Jesus, however, had been speaking about his death, but they thought that he was referring merely to sleep. [14] Then Jesus told them plainly, "Lazarus is dead. For your sake I am glad I was not there, so that you may believe. But let us go to him . . ."

[17] When Jesus arrived, he found that Lazarus had already been in the tomb four days. . . . [20] When Martha heard that Jesus was coming . . . [21] Martha said to Jesus, "Lord, if you had been here, my brother would not have died. [22] But even now I know that God will give you whatever you ask of him." [23] Jesus said to her, "Your brother will rise again. . . ."

[32] When Mary came where Jesus was and saw him, she knelt at his feet and said to him, "Lord, if you had been here, my brother would not have died." [33] When Jesus saw her weeping, and the Jews who came with her also weeping, he was greatly disturbed in spirit and deeply moved. [34] He said, "Where have you laid him?" They said to him, "Lord, come and see." [35] Jesus began to weep..."[40]

Then Jesus is greatly disturbed and goes to the tomb. At that point he calls Lazarus to come out.

And Lazarus does.

Lazarus, Martha, and Mary are all siblings and close friends of Jesus.[41] Jesus is gone and Lazarus gets sick, so Martha and Mary send word to Jesus hoping he will come heal their brother Lazarus.

When Jesus finds out about the illness, he immediately says: *"This illness does not lead to death; rather it is for God's glory, so that the Son of God may be glorified through it."[42]* Then, instead of going immediately, Jesus waits around until Lazarus dies. He then goes to see his dead friend, along with his disciples.

When Jesus arrives, Lazarus has been dead for four days. Both of Lazarus's sisters are devastated as they run to Jesus separately but cry out with the same words: *"Lord, if you had been here, my brother would not have died."[43]*

Mary falls at Jesus's feet, weeping, and *"When Jesus saw her*

weeping, and the Jews who came with her also weeping, he was greatly
disturbed in spirit and deeply moved."[44]

I can identify with the devastation and grief that Martha and
Maria must have felt, because my younger disabled brother
Jonathan also died unexpectedly. One night he just never woke
up, and in many ways the grief and pain never quite stop.

Even now, about thirteen years after Jonathan's death, I
always get emotional when I think about him.

That pain never fully goes away.

But the grief, sadness, and devastation siblings and family
members feel during the first week is almost unbearable, and it's
definitely uncontrollable. It hits you at very strange times. All of
the sudden you think you're able to keep going, but then the grief
hits you again and leaves you sobbing uncontrollably on
the floor.

That's precisely how Martha and Maria must feel only four
days after their brother died.

And incredibly, as they are on their way to Lazarus's tomb,
Jesus weeps too.[45]

Jesus weeps with them.

But then even more incredibly, when they arrive at the tomb,
Jesus orders Lazarus to come out.

And he does.

Now the question we must ask ourselves is: why on earth does
Jesus weep over the death of Lazarus?

Martha, Maria, and the others wept for the same reason
anyone weeps when a loved one dies: we are going to miss them.
We want to talk with them so bad, but we know that we can't; and
we wonder if we'll ever be able to survive without that person in
our life.

I still miss my brother Jonathan, and that's completely normal.

That explanation works for why the family and friends of Lazarus weep.

But not for Jesus.

He knows all along he is going to bring Lazarus back to life in a matter of minutes: he even announces it four different times before actually doing it![46] Jesus won't miss Lazarus because Jesus knows Lazarus will be alive again in a few minutes.

So again, why does Jesus weep in this scenario?

The only answer to that question which makes sense to me is exactly what the text says: Jesus is deeply moved and weeps. *"When Jesus saw her* [Mary] *weeping, and the Jews who came with her also weeping, he was greatly disturbed in spirit and deeply moved."*[47]

Jesus weeps when he sees his friends' intense grief, sadness, and tears.

Their pain and suffering cause him to weep.

I have studied this text and taught it for years, and that's the only conclusion I can come up with. Jesus does what good friends are supposed to do at a time like that: he supports them and has compassion on them. He walks with them through their pain, suffering, and agony, even though Jesus knows Lazarus is going to walk out of the tomb in a matter of minutes.

The kinds of friends who are able to walk through these terrible times with us are the ones we can count on in the worst, most painful moments of our lives. This is what Jesus is doing for his beloved friends, just as so many people were there for me and my family when my younger brother passed away in his sleep.

I truly believe that, without their love, support, and encouragement, we wouldn't have made it through.

And this is what Jesus does.

Even though he knows the pain and grief his friends feel won't last long, it's enough to make him feel their pain as if it were his own.

So he weeps.

With them.

Now, when disaster strikes and we are devastated, grieving, or overwhelmed, we often ask: where is God in all this pain and suffering? I asked that question a million times regarding the life and death of my brother.

Many of us think God must not really care much about us, or that God somehow is out to get us, or that he directly causes all this and then just sits back to watch us squirm.

But given the fact that, as Paul says, in Jesus we see *the image of the invisible God,* what do these tears of Jesus tell us about the heart of God?[48]

Since Jesus responds with tears to his friends' pain and suffering, we must recognize that God is immeasurably more compassionate, caring, and concerned than we give him credit for. These verses insist that we can see the heart, motives, personality, love, compassion, and fullness of God in the person of Jesus as nowhere else.

If that's true, then maybe the answer to our question is that God's heart breaks like Jesus's did when he saw his friends suffer.

Maybe God is at our side, devastated and weeping with us like Jesus did with Martha and Mary.

Maybe God cares for us so much that his own heart breaks when he sees his children grieving or suffering.

Because if Jesus reveals God to us, then in Jesus's tears we see God's heart break over our own suffering; and we can be assured that if we turn to him, he will walk with us through anything. Even if we die, he can see us through the other side of death.

How then might we turn to him?

How might we allow him to walk us through our own pain, suffering, and tears?

How might we allow him to begin to heal and restore the hurtful and broken places of our lives?

Because that's what God longs to do for everyone who turns to him.

After all, in the tears of Jesus we see the broken heart of a God who is madly in love with us.

8

THE REJECTION OF JESUS

A number of years ago, I moved to Chile for a few years to start a church called *Fuego Urbano* and reach out to the un-churched skaters, surfers, and younger generations of Chile. And one of the first skaters I met there became like a son to me.

He was an amazing young man with so much potential, but a while ago he made a few decisions that will make the rest of his life a huge struggle. He had so many hopes and dreams, but now he is just struggling to get by.

When I found out about what he's going through, I felt like someone had kicked me in the stomach or knocked the wind out of me. I was sad and heart-broken, because I knew I would have to watch this young man whom I love throw away so many of his hopes and dreams.

For the first time, I got a taste of what parents must feel when they watch their children suffer because of their bad decisions. And it was devastating.

And it got me thinking about how Jesus must have felt as he watched his children reject him and his love.

In the gospel of Luke, Jesus weeps over Jerusalem, who rejects him completely. This is fascinating, because earlier in Luke's gospel, Jesus sets out for Jerusalem declaring:

> [33] *Yet today, tomorrow, and the next day I must be on my way, because it is impossible for a prophet to be killed outside of Jerusalem.* [34] *Jerusalem, Jerusalem, the city that kills the prophets and stones those who are sent to it! How often have I desired to gather your children together as a hen gathers her brood under her wings, and you were not willing!"* [49]

While Jesus knows he will soon be killed, his disciples and the masses still do not understand what kind of king he is. The majority of the Jewish people were expecting God to send them a great anointed warrior-king who would lead them into war against Rome, defeat the Roman Empire, free the Jewish people from Roman domination, and re-establish God's reign and rule on the earth through his people.

They had a special title for the person they thought would do all that: *Messiah.*[50]

But Jesus doesn't fit into the messianic expectations of his people.

Jesus knows he's going to be killed very soon, in Jerusalem. And Jesus's words about wanting to gather Jerusalem like a hen gathers her chicks reveals how much he loves Jerusalem, and how much he longs for them to recognize that he is the one God sent to his people to save them.

In fact, farmers say that sometimes when there's a fire in a barn and everything is burned, the love and protective instinct of hens in the barns are shown when they find the burnt remains of the hens on top, but then find completely healthy chicks who took refuge from the fire under the protection of the hen's outstretched wings.

What a beautiful picture of true self-sacrificial love!

And with these words, Jesus is saying that his love for Jerusalem mirrors the love of these kinds of hens.

But tragically, Jerusalem refuses to respond to the love of Jesus, the one God sent to save them.

I can only imagine the sadness and grief Jesus must feel knowing this. He is the one God sent to save his people, but he knows they are already rejecting him and condemning themselves, and that they will continue to do so until they kill him.

Then, as Jesus is approaching Jerusalem, some fascinating things happen: the masses spread their robes on the ground in front of him, like red-carpet treatment for royalty and celebrities today; then they begin shouting, *"Blessed is the king who comes in the name of the Lord,"* referring to the messianic king God had promised to send them.[51]

Their actions imply that they believe their promised king, *Messiah*, has finally arrived.

Some Jewish religious leaders tell Jesus to quiet the crowds, but he responds that if they keep quiet, even the stones will cry out.[52] I can just imagine the excitement of the moment; the hopes of the Jewish people are finally going to be fulfilled! It should be time to party and celebrate!

But then something completely unexpected and out of place happens, in the midst of this scene of jubilation and celebration:

> [41] *As he came near and saw the city, he wept over it, saying, "If you, even you, had only recognized on this day the things that make for peace! [42] But now they are hidden from your eyes. [43] Indeed, the days will come upon you, when your enemies will set up ramparts around*

you and surround you, and hem you in on every side. 44 They will
crush you to the ground, you and your children within you, and they
will not leave within you one stone upon another; because you did not
recognize the time of your visitation from God.[53]

What?

Excuse me!

Why on earth would Jesus weep during his own parade?

The answer to that question is in the words I just quoted.
Jesus sees this great city that thinks it knows God's will for it, but
tragically gets it all wrong. Jerusalem is blind. God has sent them
their promised king and savior, the only one who can bring them
peace, but they will reject him and very soon have him executed.

And that's why Jesus weeps.

The answer to their prayers is staring them in the face, and
they don't even know it. Even the crowds who sing his praises will
soon turn on him and call for his execution. Knowing this, Jesus
weeps as he looks out over the city.

He is heart-broken.

He never wanted it to be this way.

As he said earlier, he wanted to gather, heal, and restore his
people, but they refuse.

They won't let him.

And it breaks his heart.

So he weeps.

If Jesus is the image of the invisible God, and if the fullness of
the deity dwells bodily in him, as we have seen throughout this
book, then what do Jesus's tears here reveal to us about the heart
of God?[54]

First: I believe Jesus's tears are central to the gospel because
they reveal the heart of God towards everyone, but especially

towards those who reject or deny him. God loves us deeply and wants to gather us like a hen gathers her chicks, but, tragically, we are too often unwilling.

Second: From Jesus's tears we see that the heart of God towards us—and even towards those who reject him—is one of love and compassion; it's not one of judgment, anger, or condemnation. This may come as a surprise to some people who have only heard about a God of vengeance, wrath, judgment, and condemnation, but the tears of Jesus show us the true love and compassion God has for each of us, even if we still reject or deny him.

Third: If God reveals himself to human beings most fully in the person of Jesus Christ, then we must acknowledge that God's heart breaks like Jesus's when we reject or refuse him. This means that when we reject him, he is more like a grieving parent than the cold harsh judge we tend to think of him as. Viewing God like this makes me want to honor and please him just like I want to honor and please my parents: not because I have to, but because I want to.

Fourth: God is constantly trying to break through to us. But because we have so many preconceived ideas about who God *must be*, or how God *must operate*, we are often blind to his work in our lives. We want God to fit into the tiny boxes we draw up for him, but he is way too big for our boxes. If we really want to know him at a deeper level, we must let go of our petty and small ideas and assumptions about who we think he is and allow him to be who he really is.

Fifth: As in the last chapter when we addressed the tears of Jesus, many of us look at our pain and suffering and ask: *Does God even care? Is he just cold-hearted about it?* We see the answer to these questions in Jesus's tears. God's heart breaks for us just like

Jesus's did for Jerusalem. God wants to gather us under his wings, but too often we refuse and won't let him.

Sixth: Just as Jesus was the only one God sent to save and redeem the Jewish people and the city of Jerusalem, he is also the only one who can save and redeem us. God has no *plan B*. Jesus is the one God sent to save, heal, redeem, and restore us, but we can't do it on our own. If we fail to recognize that fact, then we fall into the same trap the city of Jerusalem fell in when it rejected Jesus 2,000 years ago.

If these things about Jesus are true, then how might they change the way you think about God?

How might they reshape God's role in the midst of your own pain and suffering?

How might they change the way you view and treat others who are still rejecting the love of God?

How can you share this great news with the people in your world?

9

_____

FOOT WASHING

In John 13, Jesus sits down with his disciples on the last night he'll be with them. He starts to tell them the most important things they will need to know and remember when he's gone.

But Jesus changes things up by washing the disciples' feet. This might not seem like a big deal to us today, but back then this act carried all kinds of embarrassment, shock, and scandal.

In this chapter, we'll look at the revealing account of Jesus washing the feet of his disciples, and see what it tells us about his humanity. Here is the story:

¹ Now before the festival of the Passover, Jesus knew that his hour had come to depart from this world and go to the Father. Having loved his own who were in the world, he loved them to the end. ² The devil had already put it into the heart of Judas son of Simon Iscariot to betray him. And during supper ³ Jesus, knowing that the Father had given all things into his hands, and that he had come from God and was going to God, ⁴ got up from the table, took off his outer robe, and tied a towel around himself. ⁵ Then he poured water into a basin and began to wash the disciples' feet and to wipe them with the towel that was tied around him. ⁶ He came to Simon Peter, who said to him, "Lord, are you going to wash my feet?" ⁷Jesus answered, "You do not know now what I am doing, but later you will understand." ⁸ Peter said to him, "You will never wash my feet." Jesus answered, "Unless I wash you, you have no share with me." ⁹ Simon Peter said to him, "Lord, not my feet only but also my hands and my head!" ¹⁰ Jesus said to him, "One who has bathed does not need to wash, except for the feet, but is entirely clean. And you are clean, though not all of you." ¹¹ For he knew who was to betray him; for this reason he said, "Not all of you are clean."

*¹² After he had washed their feet, had put on his robe, and had returned to the table, he said to them, "Do you know what I have done to you? ¹³ You call me Teacher and Lord—and you are right, for that is what I am. ¹⁴ So if I, your Lord and Teacher, have washed your feet, you also ought to wash one another's feet. ¹⁵ For I have set you an example, that you also should do as I have done to you. ¹⁶ Very truly, I tell you, servants are not greater than their master, nor are messengers greater than the one who sent them. ¹⁷ If you know these things, you are blessed if you do them. ¹⁸ I am not speaking of all of you; I know whom I have chosen. But it is to fulfill the scripture, 'The one who ate my bread has lifted his heel against me.' ¹⁹I tell you this now, before it occurs, so that when it does occur, you may believe that I am he. ²⁰ Very truly, I tell you, whoever receives one whom I send receives me; and whoever receives me receives him who sent me."*⁵⁵

In the first century, Jewish men wore long robes that covered their bodies and helped protect them from getting dirty. Because of this, feet were the dirtiest part of the body. We need to remember that they wore open-toed sandals, and they constantly went walking through the fields and streets.

They didn't have clean sidewalks. They walked along roads of dirt and worked in fields and homes made largely of dirt. Most people had agriculture and farm animals, too, so they were constantly walking and working in the dirt, along with the feces those animals left behind every day. Because of all this, the open-toed sandals they wore would allow all the dirt, filth, mud, sweat, and feces to stick to the feet of everyone.

If a Jewish man owned a house or land, he probably would have also had a servant or two. And when the man, or lord, of the house came home, whose job do you think it was to wash the feet of the owner or lord of the house?

It wasn't his job. And it wasn't the job of anyone in his family either, because it was viewed as too degrading.

It was the job of the servant because it was so dirty, humiliating, and shameful.

Never in a million years would a king, or any member of royalty, wash someone's feet. Most kings from that time would have probably preferred death to being forced to wash the feet of another person, and even more so in public. Now, let's look at the account again:

In verse 1, it says: *"Having loved his own who were in the world, he loved them to the end."*[56] How does Jesus love his disciples to the end? By doing what we are about to unpack so we can understand how scandalous his actions are.

Verse 3 says: *"Jesus, knowing that the Father had given all things into his hands, and that he had come from God and was going to God. . ."*[57] What does this mean? It means Jesus knew God put everything under Jesus's authority, including all his disciples in the room with him. He also knew that he came from God, and was now returning to God.

In other words, Jesus knows the Father has given all things to him. By all things, he means every person, nation, ruler, animal, and thing in all of creation. It means Jesus knows exactly who he is, who he's called to be, and what he's called to do. He knows that he came from God and is returning to God, and all this comes from God.

And because of this, Jesus doesn't have to try and prove his worth, identity, or value to anyone, because these are grounded in his relationship with his Father. As long as that's good, then he can give himself away by serving other people, without worrying about how his actions make him appear to others.

That's the stupid game we always get stuck in because we try to prove to everyone—including ourselves—just how worthy of respect, greatness, applause, honor, congratulations, recognition, acceptance, approval, fame, and lots of other things we are.

But Jesus doesn't play that game, because he knows he gets all those things from his father.

That's why Jesus is able to stoop so low and perform the job of a servant in a way most of us can't.

I say *can't* not because it's impossible for us to do, but because normally we are so worried about our honor, dignity, pride, and reputation that we will never be able to give ourselves away in service to other people like Jesus. As long as we care primarily about what others say and think about us, instead of what God says and thinks about us, this kind of self-humiliation will seem impossible for us.

But when we are able to ground our identity, value, and worth in our relationship with our father, as Jesus does here, we'll find that we stop caring about what other people think or say about us. We'll be truly free to give ourselves away in ways that leave people in awe. After all, that's exactly what Jesus does in this passage.

Then in verses 6–8, Peter sees Jesus performing this demeaning and shameful act, and he wants no part of it.

Just a few chapters earlier in John's gospel, when the disciples were on their way to Jerusalem, Peter correctly said Jesus was the *Christos*, which is the Greek word for Messiah.

Messiah was supposed to be a king used by God to reestablish the Kingdom of God on the earth forever. So now, Peter sees this king, Messiah Jesus, performing the shameful and degrading job of a servant.

Peter knows kings in the ancient world are all about preserving power, authority, and pride, as well as about showing everyone how powerful they are. There's nothing in Peter's thinking that can make sense of the fact that Messiah Jesus, or King Jesus, is preforming the job of a slave.

In fact, all power and authority were given to Jesus by his Father, so if anyone has a right to cling to those things, it is Jesus.

But he doesn't.

Instead, he humbles himself and performs the job of a slave.

And he can only do that because his identity is grounded in the approval of his father, and not in the approval of the men who are in the room with him.

Eventually, Peter gives in and lets Jesus wash his feet. Then Jesus tells them he gave them an example he wants them to follow. It's as if Jesus is saying to them, and to us, "Look, I have every right to command you to wash my feet because of who I am, but I've never used my position to secure my rights. My whole way of living is by giving up the very things that I have every right to claim for myself, so I can serve the people who don't deserve it."

Jesus means for our lives to look like his when he stoops down to wash his disciples' feet. The posture and attitude of our

lives should look like him stooping down to perform the shameful, embarrassing, act of a servant. Because if Jesus, who is a king,
is willing to stoop that low, then we who aren't kings have no
excuse for not following his example.

Knowing our identity and worth as God's children will free us
to serve, give, sacrifice, and humble ourselves, without worrying
about what other people think of us. We will only be able to do
this when we know where we come from, and where we're going,
just like Jesus.

Otherwise we'll keep trying to seek after things like power,
prestige, applause, recognition, fame, respect, gratitude,
and honor.

So how is God calling you to humble yourself and serve
like Jesus?

And what's keeping you from doing that right now?

10

KEEPING IT TOGETHER IN GETHSEMANE

There are a few people in my life who I absolutely love being around because, no matter how difficult things get, they always seem to reassure me that everything is going to be okay. They are like my own personal team of heroes who seem to save the day merely by their presence, smiles, laughter, or voices.

However, I can recall many times when a few of those people I have looked to for comfort and reassurance were on the verge of breaking down, and I remember thinking: *if this person is breaking down, am I going to be okay?*

After all, if the person we look to for reassurance and strength is barely holding things together, then what does that say about those of us who depend on that person to hold us together?

Shockingly, I think Jesus's disciples experienced this in Gethsemane.

After a few years of ministry, Jesus arrived at Jerusalem with his disciples. It is impossible to know how much Jesus knew about his future, but he clearly had an awareness that he would suffer and die in Jerusalem, be raised three days later, and that this would ransom many people from bondage into freedom.

After arriving in Jerusalem, he eventually gathered with his disciples for one last dinner—a Jewish Passover meal. The Passover was an annual dinner-celebration meant to remind the Jews about how God had freed them from slavery in Egypt by sending an angel of death to kill the first-born sons there. It was also to remind them how the first-born sons of the Jews were spared by having their parents kill an unblemished lamb and smear its blood on their doorposts. The angel of death passed over the houses of the Jews and did not harm any of their sons.

Drawing from these shared Jewish images, Jesus began to explain to them that the Passover they were about to celebrate would be different because it would be his own blood that would be poured out on their behalf.

After eating, they walked over to the Mount of Olives where Jesus announced to them that their shepherd was about to be struck down, and that they would all fall away and scatter. Peter objected to this and insisted he would remain faithful, even to the point of death, but Jesus responded by announcing in front of everyone that Peter would disown Jesus three times before the night was over.

After this, Jesus headed to a nearby garden called Gethsemane.

When Jesus arrived at the Garden of Gethsemane, he wanted to get away to pray. He took with him Peter, James, and John, and left the other disciples behind. Matthew describes the scene:

> [37] He took with him Peter and the two sons of Zebedee, and began to be grieved and agitated. [38] Then he said to them, "I am deeply grieved, even to death; remain here, and stay awake with me." [39] And going a

little farther, he threw himself on the ground and prayed, "My Father, if it is possible, let this cup pass from me; yet not what I want but what you want." ⁴⁰ Then he came to the disciples and found them sleeping; and he said to Peter, "So, could you not stay awake with me one hour? ⁴¹ Stay awake and pray that you may not come into the time of trial; the spirit indeed is willing, but the flesh is weak." ⁴² Again he went away for the second time and prayed, "My Father, if this cannot pass unless I drink it, your will be done." ⁴³ Again he came and found them sleeping, for their eyes were heavy. ⁴⁴ So leaving them again, he went away and prayed for the third time, saying the same words. ⁴⁵ Then he came to the disciples and said to them, "Are you still sleeping and taking your rest? See, the hour is at hand, and the Son of Man is betrayed into the hands of sinners. ⁴⁶ Get up, let us be going. See, my betrayer is at hand."[58]

What stands out to me first is the depth and authenticity of Jesus's anguish, fear, and sorrow. He describes himself as being deeply grieved and overwhelmed, to the point of death.[59] In fact, Luke says Jesus is so anguished that, *"his sweat became like great drops of blood falling down on the ground."*[60]

Many people read about the sweat and blood and automatically discredit Luke as inventing fantasies here, but modern medicine has now classified that condition as *hematidrosis*, which is a rare medical condition caused by severe psychological stress.

We can't be sure exactly what Jesus means when he says he is *"deeply grieved, even to death,"* but we can be sure that this was no joke.

Jesus is not faking.

He is doing everything in his power to keep it all together.

Maybe that is why he takes Peter, James, and John along with him while leaving the other disciples behind. He probably does not want the others to see him like that. They probably would have freaked out and panicked, so he takes only his closest friends for his own personal comfort.

Jesus is completely overwhelmed.

To the point of death.

The second thing that stands out about this is that Jesus once again reveals that he does not know everything and must therefore decide if he will trust in the goodness of his father's will or not. It is obvious from his own words that while he knows a lot about what is going to happen, he does not know everything.

He says, "*My Father, if it is possible, let this cup pass from me; yet not what I want but what you want.*" The words '*if it is possible*' necessarily imply that Jesus does not know if what he is about to ask is possible. He hopes it is possible, but does not know for sure.

If it is possible for him to avoid this bitter cup of suffering and still save the world he came to save, then he would like to do it; but if it is not possible, he is willing to deny his own will and submit to his father's will.

This is absolutely stunning.

Jesus is being forced, like you and I every day, to face an uncertain future and trust in the goodness of his father's will, even when it means doing something Jesus himself does not want to do. Jesus is asking his father for deliverance—to save him from his suffering if there is any other way to save us.

But here, Jesus experiences what you and I also experience from God, which is the answer: *No. I'm sorry son. Not this time.*

Maybe Jesus is hoping this will be another Abraham and Isaac story. God tested Abraham by telling him to sacrifice his son, but actually had no intention of letting Abraham go through with the killing, intervening in the end by providing a lamb for Abraham to sacrifice instead.

Maybe Jesus hopes his father will intervene in the end, like he did with Abraham and Isaac.

But this time there will be no intervention.

There is no other way.

Jesus is the sacrificial lamb.

In this story, the son must die.

So how does this aspect of Jesus's humanity affect the way we view him? We admire war heroes who throw themselves on top of grenades in order to save others, because we know they had to deny their own will for self-preservation in order to do what they did not want to do. That is why people honor and adore them.

This is Jesus throwing himself on top of the grenade to save us.

That's love.

That's my hero.

How might this change the way you think about the sacrifice and suffering Jesus had to endure in order to set you free?

How will you respond to such a breathtaking demonstration of selfless love?

FORSAKEN

On March 3, 1991, a number of LAPD police officers were video-taped savagely beating African-American motorist Rodney King with their Billy clubs after he led them on a high-speed chase. When they finally caught him, all the officers gathered around and beat him senseless, almost killing him.

I remember my stomach turning inside-out every time I watched that video, because the officers continued to strike King again and again, even though he had long since stopped moving.

As bad as that was, it turns my stomach even more to think that, in Jesus, the creator of the universe willingly submitted himself to something even worse.

We Protestants don't like to dwell on Jesus's suffering or the fact that he was beaten and crucified. It makes us uncomfortable. We prefer to skip right over those dark details and get right to Easter, leaving Jesus's agony, suffering, and passion for the Catholics to ponder.

We see evidence of this in the different crosses Protestants and Catholics use. Protestants use bare crosses, but Catholics almost always use crosses that have the body of Jesus hanging on them.

But I think we Protestants need to take a lesson from our Catholic brothers and sisters. We should pause so that we might soak in, perhaps for the first time, what Jesus had to endure during his very human suffering and crucifixion. Otherwise, we won't be able to fully appreciate the sacrifice he made on our behalf, and we might be tempted to take it for granted.

Mark 15:15 says this about Pilate and Jesus: *"After flogging Jesus, he handed him over to be crucified."*[61] We tend to run right past the word *flogging*, figuring they must have given Jesus a few good whacks on his back-side. But this was something completely different.

Roman floggings were done with large, braided, leather whips that had lots of metal balls (which were meant to bruise) and sharp stones and bones (which were meant to slice like a razor) woven into them, in order to cause maximum pain and suffering on the people they flogged.

It was believed 40 lashes would kill someone, so to avoid this, standard floggings consisted of 39 lashes; but often the wounds on the victim's back were so deep, their spine would be exposed.

Unfortunately for Jesus, this flogging was only the beginning.

After being flogged, Jesus was handed over to the Roman soldiers to be crucified. Like watching the Rodney King beating, reading this turns my stomach; but I need to read it to feel the weight of what Jesus went through:

> [16] *Then the soldiers led him into the courtyard of the palace (that is, the governor's headquarters); and they called together the whole cohort.* [17] *And they clothed him in a purple cloak; and after twisting some thorns into a crown, they put it on him.* [18] *And they began*

saluting him, "Hail, King of the Jews!" [19] *They struck his head with a reed, spat upon him, and knelt down in homage to him.* [20] *After mocking him, they stripped him of the purple cloak and put his own clothes on him. Then they led him out to crucify him.* [62]

This scene is revolting. The whole company of soldiers gather around Jesus, like the Rodney King beating, but they don't want to just punish him; they want to absolutely humiliate him. Since he is supposed to be a king, the soldiers decide dress him up like one. They put him in a purple robe, which was the color of royalty, and then they shove a thorned crown onto his head.

They make fun of him by falling on their knees and pretending to pay homage to him, all the while striking his head over and over again with their staff. The thorns on Jesus's crown would have been about as long as human fingers, so every time the soldiers strike him on the head, the thorns sink deeper and deeper into Jesus's head.

As if that were not enough, they spit on him for good measure.

At this point they lead him out *"to crucify him,"* which is another loaded term we prefer to skip over, but need to unpack. Crucifixion was so gruesome and painful that the Romans did not have a word to describe it, so they invented a new one: *excrux*, which means "from/out of the cross" in Latin. We now use it in the word *excruciating*.

It was so savage that it was never mentioned in polite Roman society, and Roman citizens were exempt from it.

The purpose was not to merely kill. The purpose was to kill someone publicly by using the slowest, most painful, and agonizing process possible, so that everyone could see what happened when thieves and revolutionaries rebelled against Roman authority.

That is why Romans always crucified people in public, where everyone could see them. The purpose was to send a message so terrifying that anyone who saw someone crucified would be scared into never rebelling against Rome.

It was the ultimate public humiliation and execution.

Victims, including Jesus, were stripped completely naked, which means there were no cloths covering his private parts like we see on the crucified Jesus of statues and images today. And then they were hung on the cross by having huge 6-inch nails driven through their wrists and ankles.

As painful as the nails were, they would not kill the victim.

The victim would die of suffocation, normally after a day or two on the cross. In order to keep breathing, the victim would need to lift up on their legs enough to allow them to exhale before collapsing back down. At a certain point, the victim would be too exhausted to lift their body anymore, and at that point, the person would die from suffocation.

The reason Jesus died in about 6 hours, which was very quick for a crucifixion, was because he had been so severely flogged and beaten before that he was barely alive when they crucified him.

What's amazing is that even after being flogged 39 times, beaten to a pulp by a whole company of Roman soldiers, and then crucified, Jesus was forced to endure even more insults:

> [29] Those who passed by derided him, shaking their heads and saying, "Aha! You who would destroy the temple and build it in three days, [30] save yourself, and come down from the cross!" [31] In the same way the chief priests, along with the scribes, were also mocking him among

themselves and saying, "He saved others; he cannot save himself. 32
Let the Messiah, the King of Israel, come down from the cross now, so
that we may see and believe." Those who were crucified with him also
taunted him.[63]

The tragically ironic thing about this scene is that if Jesus wanted to rescue human beings from our own sin and death, the one thing he could not do was come down off the cross. The fact that he chose to endure all this leaves me speechless.

May we never take the suffering and sacrifice of Jesus lightly.

May we never think the gift of God's grace was free.

It came at a heavy price that Jesus paid, so we wouldn't have to.

May we never turn God's grace into *cheap grace*, where we do not really grasp, value, or appreciate what Jesus did for us.

Instead, let us live our lives in light of the heavy price that was paid on our behalf, making every day count as we live for the one who lived, suffered, and died, for us.

In becoming human, Jesus took on our humanity, but without our sin. Here, at the cross, for the first time he took on the sin of the whole world.

He didn't sin and wasn't deserving of this death.

We are the ones who sinned.

We should be on the cross.

If this is true, then how can we say *no* to Jesus?

What else could he do to show and prove his love for us?

How will you respond?

II

THE NEW CHRISTIAN OBSESSION: CHASING AN UPWARD TRAJECTORY

12

SLAVES TO THE AMERICAN DREAM

At this point, you might be wondering what's the big deal about everything I've said so far about the humanity of Jesus. Other than helping to show how far Jesus humbled and emptied himself for us, and helping us to more fully appreciate what he did, what's the big deal?

Does this affect our lives in any way?

Yes!

If we take what the New Testament tells us about Jesus seriously—especially Paul's words in Philippians 2:5-11 about Jesus emptying and humbling himself when he took on human form— then we will be forced to recognize that the overall downward motion of *God-Jesus-us* contradicts the overall upward movement and motion of the *American Dream*.

Jesus humbling and emptying himself of parts of his divine nature to reach and save you and I was an overall downward trajectory from God, to Jesus, and then to us. Jesus willingly set aside all kinds of divine rights, attributes, and characteristics when he became human, and he did all that so he could meet us where we are, to reach and save us.

The overall trajectory, attitude, and actions of Jesus was consistently downward.

But the American Dream, which is the air we breathe and the food we eat in our country, moves in the opposite direction.

It moves upward.

By the American Dream, I refer to the way we have been told that nothing can stop us from ascending up the ladders of our society. These ladders are social, professional, personal, economic, and just about any other things you can dream up.

Unfortunately, the vast majority of American Christians follow the American dream, which means the overall trajectory of our lives is moving in the opposite direction as that of Jesus.

This leaves Christians in a state of not being able to recognize and help people through the difficulties of life, when things gets really hard. We don't want to accompany people down into the trenches of the things they are battling against, because that would interfere with our ever-ascending lives, plans, hopes, and dreams.

But the downward trajectory of Jesus forces us to walk with people in the lowly places they happen to live. We are forced to walk with people in areas of sadness, grief, emotional pain, abuse, physical pain, sickness, mental health issues, disease, poverty, divorce, death, oppression, and lots of other things we could add to this list.

The downward trajectory of the life of Jesus leads us to embrace the tough realities of life, and that means walking with people through tough things they're going through. It teaches us to prepare for those challenges, and helps us to more fully identify with the people going through them.

Triumphalist Christianity

When we follow the upward trajectory of the American Dream, instead of the downward trajectory of the life of Jesus, we fall into a shallow triumphalist Christianity that refuses to acknowledge the real pain and suffering we all go through at some point in our lives.

This failure to recognize and live through the hurt and pain of these realities leaves American Christians unable to walk through their own pain and suffering, and unable to help other people walk through the pain and suffering they go through. It leaves American Christians incapable of embracing the difficult realities that life will inevitably force us to confront at some point.

As Americans, we're told we can do anything.

We're told the sky is the limit to our potential.

Now, to some degree, this is true. We all believe this, and we all more or less live by that value. But my question is this: as followers of Jesus who are called to follow him first and foremost, *should we really be concerned with climbing all these ladders* so we reach a higher social, personal, professional, or economic level?

I question this even more when we take into account the unstated assumption about these things. This is the assumption that, in order to ascend into these new social, personal, professional, and economic levels, we must be willing to compete and win against any of our rivals who are trying to do the same thing. In fact, the competition is often so fierce that, in order to ascend, we must be willing to try to cut down or eliminate our rivals.

Those environments seek after things like money, wealth, power, recognition, fame, notoriety, praise, adulation, compliments, and many other things we human beings love to seek after.

But none of these things have anything to do with the self-humbling and emptying attitude of Jesus that Paul says we should have. If this is true, then how can we justify this constant upward motion if we are followers of Jesus, since his whole life was spent not ascending, but descending to meet us right where we are?

How can we do this, especially in light of the fact that the whole reason Paul writes his amazing words in Philippians 2:5–11, is so that we will have the same mind, or attitude, as Christ?[64] This is why Paul says:

> [5] *Let the same mind be in you that was in Christ Jesus,* [6] *who, though he was in the form of God, did not regard equality with God as something to be exploited,* [7] *but emptied himself, taking the form of a slave, being born in human likeness. And being found in human form,* [8] *he humbled himself and became obedient to the point of death— even death on a cross.*
>
> [9] *Therefore God also highly exalted him and gave him the name that is above every name,* [10] *so that at the name of Jesus every knee should bend, in heaven and on earth and under the earth,* [11] *and every tongue should confess that Jesus Christ is Lord, to the glory of God the Father.*[65]

That means Paul expects us to follow the model of Jesus, so we too should empty and humble ourselves to seek and save the lost. William Dyrness describes the American dream, and the Christian response to it, like this:

The future is . . . bright with promise, the past is something to be outgrown and discarded. All of life is believed to favor the boundless optimism of . . . a present full of possibilities and hope.

But problems arise. . . . The past is given no intrinsic value, outside of its preparation for today. As a result, evil and tragedy have no place; we certainly are not responsible for them. . . . The . . . irony . . . is that . . . hopefulness has now become . . . an obstacle to genuine faith. . . .

It is not hard to see why . . . victorious Christianity has become the primary language of evangelicalism. . . . Hope is a wonderful gift, and . . . it can be used to point people to the source of that hope. But when people . . . follow Christ, they must learn that discipleship involves . . . bearing . . . the cross— sharing the pain and brokenness of the fallen order. . . .

What if, after all, we do not succeed? What if . . . we fail? . . . The other side of our irrepressible hope . . . is disillusionment. Perhaps the deep cynicism among certain segments of our society . . . is simply the dark side of our cultural hopefulness. When the dream is not fulfilled, there is nothing to live for. . . .

Americans are a people of . . . privilege, not . . . need. We are imbued with an expectation of success, not an awareness of failure. This means we . . . cannot deal well with suffering and death . . . that we dangerously misinterpret the gospel. For in it the way to live must always be through death. . . . real hope comes only through death.[66]

There are a number of things I want to draw our attention to about this quote regarding how our American culture has affected American Christianity. First, the American way of thinking is so positive and triumphalist that our Christianity comes off that way, too. Evidence of this is in the way we forget the past and disregard it.

In fact, we fail to recognize evils from the past because we are so hopeful and positive about the future. We deny evil and blame it on past generations, and then place all our faith and hope in the future, which we're convinced will be much better than the past.

The greatest irony is that our insatiable hopefulness, and our positive and triumphal faith and attitudes, become hindrances to genuine faith in Jesus. How do we know this is true? There are a few things we can look at. For example, the language of victorious Christianity has become the language we use when we want to evangelize or share our faith. We talk about how much God loves people, and that he has an amazing plan for their lives.

Hope is good when it leads us to the source of our hope, but we often fail to tell people the reality of what following Jesus entails: carrying our crosses daily to follow Jesus.

Carrying our crosses isn't fun, but we're all called to do it.

Jesus will inevitably lead us to places we don't want to go, but we don't tell people that when we explain the gospel.

We also need to remember what God has done for us, because we will inevitably be greatly disappointed if we go out with all the good hopes in the world, but then are confronted with the reality of what happens when we fail to live up to those great hopes.

In fact, some of the darkest parts of our society can be explained by people who started out with so much optimism and hope but were then left to pick up the pieces when they failed to attain what they hoped for.

Dyrness says people who are comfortable, which is the vast majority of the people in our country, normally don't cry out to

God for help. They don't cry out to God because they don't think they need to. They think they're just fine, and they don't see themselves as needing anything from God.

In contrast, the people who suffer, while not necessarily being saved because of it, tend to be able to recognize their need and open themselves up to God.

But once again, our whole country is so incredibly based on hapless optimism and comfort that we often fail to recognize our own need for anything.

The American ethos, or attitude, is one that celebrates and embraces things like success, privilege, victory, and triumphs. In fact, we do this so much that we don't know how to deal with things like pain, suffering, or death.

And because of this, we misinterpret the gospel.

Since we are called to follow and emulate Jesus, who was crucified for us, the gospel entails suffering and death. We are called to carry our crosses daily, which means we have to learn to put to death certain parts of our lives to follow Jesus.

In fact, I've seen how the faith of Christians in Latin America is different from the faith of Christians in the USA. Christians in Latin America understand sadness, grief, suffering, and death. They learn to embrace and embody these aspects in very beautiful and powerful ways. But the vast majority of American Christians are simply unable to do this because we don't know how to come to terms with any of these things.

We don't know how to suffer or grieve.

We don't know how to carry our crosses.

We don't know how to follow Jesus.

A Different Way

What would it look like if we were really humbling and emptying ourselves like Jesus? I'll give you a few examples from my past, beginning with a feeding program I helped start at the church where I did college and young adult ministry for three years before moving to Chile.

There is a very big homeless population in Huntington Beach. When I got hired at this church, the way they helped the homeless and hungry was by providing one sacked lunch per week to each person. The people would come upstairs and ask for the lunch, which came in brown paper bags, and then they would leave and not come back until the next week.

That was better than doing nothing at all, but I started thinking we could do much more than that.

Up until this point, the hungry people would come up to ask for their lunch, and then they would get it and leave. Everything was nice and cordial, but no one was getting to know one another, and there was zero relationship happening on either side.

It was almost like when we go into a bank to get a transaction done. You're nice, and everyone treats you well, but once you finish the transaction, you're gone. That was how this particular feeding policy appeared to me.

But in our staff meetings, I suggested that we rethink that policy, and challenged us to think of what Jesus would do if he were us. I told them that I kept thinking Jesus would invite them in, having them sit down and eat together. Jesus would eat with them so he could talk with them and get to know them. He would welcome them and affirm their dignity as human beings, so that's what I wanted to move us towards.

After praying about this idea with the staff, we shared the vision with the whole church a couple Sundays later, inviting everyone who was interested in volunteering to come to a meeting after the morning services. We had no idea how many people would want to volunteer, but we were going to be really excited if we got 15–20 people to commit to making food for the homeless and hungry on Sunday afternoons (we decided on Sunday afternoons because typical feeding programs are closed then).

When we had the meeting, about 130 people showed up wanting to volunteer!

We were absolutely blown away. So, instead of us being there each week to prepare the food and care for the people, we divided everyone into five teams of about 25 people on each team. We decided to rotate each Sunday, so each team served once every five weeks.

The teams were (and still are) responsible for their own menus, and they all cooked massive meals that included meats, pastas, casseroles, salads, and the obligatory desserts of cakes, pies, and ice creams.

We wanted to create a place where everyone felt welcome and respected, so we also made a point of having team members welcome people at the door and write the names of the guests on nametags so we could all address people by name.

We also encouraged the teams to eat with the people we served in order to get to know them. So when it came time to eat, usually about a third of the team members would grab a plate and eat with everyone else at the tables.

Then we decided to send out everyone who came with sacked lunches to eat during Sunday night and Monday morning. Within a few weeks, people heard about how amazing the food and atmosphere was; ever since, there have been about 70–90 people who come to eat and hang out together.

We wanted that ministry to be a place where these people feel welcome and affirmed for who they are, because for many of them, they don't get that anywhere else. In fact, the people who come to eat love it so much that they get there early to help set up all the tables and food. They also stay late to help clean up and vacuum, and they quickly regulate themselves whenever there are problems or issues with anyone there.

In fact, we started that ministry about seven years ago. When it hit its fifth year anniversary, the city of Huntington Beach gave the church a plaque of recognition that honored them for serving the homeless and hungry of our city so faithfully for those five years.

How could you empty and humble yourself to serve the needy people of your community?

Yet Another Way

Another example of how we can follow the top-to-bottom movement of Jesus is in a different ministry I helped connect that same church with. I helped the church set up an official relationship between our church and an organization in Guatemala. This organization shared the gospel by providing wheel chairs and building homes for people who were handicapped or disabled.

The ministry down there is amazing, and the family who run it are incredible. They have lived there for about 15 years, and have dedicated themselves to sharing the gospel by putting the words of Jesus into action in Guatemala. Everyone in Guatemala is much poorer than the people in the USA, but the poorest of the poor are the handicapped and disabled people, and that's why this family serves them.

Unfortunately, most people in Guatemala lack the resources to get a wheelchair for a family member who is disabled. Most disabled people there live their lives locked up inside a house, lying on the floor.

Almost none of them ever get to experience the mobility and new life of something so simple as a wheelchair. But this family has dedicated their lives to bringing people the Gospel through their outreaches by providing wheelchairs to the poorest of the poor.

They have been doing this for a long time, but, more recently, they were able to start building homes for the disabled people who don't have any adequate housing. This amazing American family has devoted their lives to humbling themselves and meeting the disabled people of Guatemala right where they are.

When we went down there to set up our commitment to one another, we were all really excited. We told them we thought we could probably get 3–4 teams down there each year, which would build about six to eight houses per year, as well as help distribute hundreds of wheelchairs.

When I think of what it looks like to empty and humble ourselves like Jesus did, I think about these kinds of people. This family has devoted their whole lives to serving the poorest of the poor, including the most vulnerable people anywhere in Guatemala.

What is stopping you from following their example?

One More Vision

While I love the example of this family who serves the disabled people of Guatemala, I want to finish this section by giving another example of how we can put into practice the emptying and humbling of ourselves in our communities.

One way we can do this in our communities is by partnering with schools that are in the toughest areas of where you live. A final program I helped start at the church in Huntington Beach was a school-adoption program. We decided we were going to adopt two elementary schools and the local high school, committing ourselves to loving, supporting, and serving them by helping them fill whatever needs they had.

For example, if they needed tutors, we found people from our church who could do it. If they needed manual labor done on the schools, like painting, power-blasting, gum scraping, or other cleaning, we did it. If teachers needed volunteers in the classes to help support certain needs they had, we found them from our congregation. If they needed backpacks and school supplies for their lower-income students, we provided them.

There is literally no end to these kinds of needs, but when churches choose to adopt the schools in their neighborhood, and especially the lower-income schools in the worst neighborhoods, that speaks volumes to the school staff and the whole community. Most people call schools to get something from them, but almost no one reaches out to them simply to bless them by helping them with whatever they need.

Those kinds actions and attitudes truly embody the self-emptying and humbling that Jesus lived out and calls us to. When we take the time to humble ourselves in order to serve the schools in our communities, the school staff, as well as all the parents of everyone who goes to that school, are absolutely stunned.

They are blown away.

And they immediately want to know what it is that causes us to humble ourselves and serve them so passionately.

Our answer will always be Jesus.

So how can you humble and empty yourself to serve the people in your world?

13

BIG-FACE WORSHIP

When we fall into a shallow, triumphalist faith, it leaves Christians without the tools to walk through the tough times of life with our faith intact. It produces the kind of cheery faith that only works when things are great, but which falls apart when we're going through tough times.

I call this shallow faith *Big-Face Worship.*

Big-Face Worship is the kind of happy-go-lucky faith that is all about joy, smiles, laughs, and fun. It's the kind used by lots of megachurches, which often have a choir up front where everyone is dressed impeccably, smiling the whole time they are singing.

The reason I call it Big-Face Worship is because they often have people filming the faces of the choir members, which they then project on their huge screens in front of the church. That way, everyone can see the close-ups of these big happy faces, smiling and singing as if they don't have a care in the world.

My problem with this kind of worship and Christianity is: what happens when our lives fall apart?

What happens when we suffer real tragedy, sorrow, or grief?

What happens when we can barely keep going?

What happens when your younger brother is so severely mentally and physically handicapped that he can't do anything on his own, and your family has to care for him 24 hours a day, 7 days a week, because no one else knows what he needs?

What happens when your severely handicapped brother is too big for your family to care for anymore, so after eight years of taking care of him, you bring him to a home where he's going to live the rest of his life; and as you leave you hear him screaming bloody murder because for eight years he's never been away from his family, and now because of the laws of his new home, you won't be able to see him for months?

What happens when, as you walk away from the home you were forced to leave your brother in, where he will live the rest of his life, you feel like the worst brother on earth, and like you just betrayed your own flesh and blood?

What happens when that feeling of betraying and failing your younger brother never leaves you, but gnaws at you constantly for the rest of your life?

What happens when you deliberately turn your back on God for 10 years because you see no evidence of his love and goodness in your life, and because the church you grew up in, who supported your family through all those hard times, turns its back on your family and wants nothing to do with you?

What happens when you have to work on weekends doing construction with your dad because you need to make more money for your family, since your whole family, including your severely handicapped brother with his astronomical medical bills, are living off one construction salary?

What happens when your family is so poor that you always

have old piece of crap cars, and all your friends make fun of you whenever they see them?

What happens when your family is barely making it, and you need to move so much just to survive that by the time you finish your first year of high school, you've lived in seven different houses and had to make all new friends every time except the last two?

What happens when your family is so far in debt that you're forced to declare bankruptcy and move in with your grandma, because your family can't pay the bills after years of trying to keep up?

What happens when your severely handicapped younger brother dies in his sleep one night, and you didn't even get a chance to hug him, kiss him, say good-bye, or tell him you love him one more time?

What happens if your dad goes in for a standard MRI to make sure nothing is wrong with his neck, but he's so claustrophobic that he has a massive panic attack; has a brain aneurism; and from then on is a shadow of the person he was before, never able to work or socialize in any meaningful way?

What happens when the guy who was the heart and soul of the college ministry you used to lead gets cancer and dies before he's 25 years old, leaving you with a huge void in your heart and life?

What happens if, while you're trying to help your dad recover from his brain aneurism, you find out that your dad has Huntington's Disease, which has the physical symptoms of Parkinson's, but from a different cause?

What happens if you do tests and find out you inherit Huntington's Disease from your dad, and that while there is progress being made towards a cure, today there still is no cure for it?

What happens when you have to watch your dad waste away in a home for the elderly, even though he's only 69, because he can't talk or take care of himself due to the damage from his brain aneurism, two brain surgeries, and Huntington's Disease?

What happens when your dad falls down and hurts himself severely, and the doctors put him on hospice care and only give him one to two more weeks to live?

What happens when you take him home to love him and surround him with family and friends for his last few days, but there is no way to avoid the fact that you are forced to say good-bye to your dad way too soon?

These are all things that have happened in my own life. I don't tell you these things so you'll feel sorry for me. I tell you this because I'm just one person, and if I've had to deal with all this pain, sadness, grief, and suffering in my life, then just imagine what other people have gone through. My story is just one story, but there are plenty of people who have suffered much more than I have.

What does this shallow Big-Face Worship and Christianity have to say to the people who have been through things like divorces?

Or to people whose parents died when they were young?

Or to people who have been molested or raped?

What does it have to say to people who are addicted to drugs or alcohol?

If the Gospel is only good news for the people who are joyful and happy, then it's not actually good news at all. The only way the Gospel can be the truly great news I'm convinced it is is if it's good news for everyone, no matter how we feel.

That means it's good news when we're joyful and happy, but also when we're hurting and suffering.

It's good news when things are going great and when things are going terrible.

It's even good news when things are just fine, but not better or worse than that.

The good news of Jesus is for everyone, no matter what we're dealing with or how we're feeling.

The reason I hate this shallow Big-Face Worship is because it doesn't have anything to say to us when we suffer. When we're hurting, those gatherings of so-called happiness and smiles seem like nothing more than pretentious lies.

How can we be forced to be happy when we're not happy?

How can we be forced to happy when we're sad and hurting?

Churches and Christians that subscribe to Big-Face Worship make everyone else think we should all be as happy as they are; and if we're not, then there must be something wrong with our faith.

What is someone like me, who has experienced serious pain and suffering, supposed to say to those kinds of people?

Nothing.

And if you want to know the truth, Big-Faced Christians kept me away from Jesus for a long time, because I thought I needed to be happy like them before I could go to church. I thought I needed to either get everything together, or fake like I had everything together, before I would be welcome at church. And since I couldn't do either of those things, I stayed away from Jesus and the church even longer than I would have if those people were not like that.

Nowhere does Jesus say following him will be easy. In fact, throughout the gospels, he makes the exact opposite point. Over and over again he says that following him is going to be really hard, so we should weigh the cost before saying yes to him. I'm okay with that, and I really admire church communities that embrace all of life, both the good and the bad.

These kinds of Christians and churches tend to be deep and battered by the harsh realities and battles of life. We know that, in the end, Jesus has ensured us victory, but that doesn't mean we can avoid or deny the very real pain, suffering, or sadness we may be feeling right now.

When churches fall into shallow Big-Faced Worship, it is truly poisonous and toxic. Any kind of faith that requires us to deny our reality is set to fail from the start.

It's like Paul's idea when he says we grieve, but not as those without hope.[67] Therefore, we suffer the realities of our lives, but never give in to the cynicism and hopelessness that non-Christians so easily fall into. According to Paul, we should grieve and suffer, but not without hope.

But people and churches who embrace Big-Face Worship refuse to allow people the space to grieve or suffer.

They live in denial.

And they think they're being spiritual or mature.

But they're not.

Big-Faced Worship denies reality and says: *Don't worry! Be Happy!*

That's great advice if you're a reggae band in the 1980's and you want a catchy song title to make a hit out of; but it's not good advice if you try to live by it, or if you try to make everyone else live by it. Sometimes—in fact, most times—life just isn't that carefree and happy. And to pretend that it is is to be disingenuous and deceive ourselves.

We can't pretend to feel one way when we simply don't feel like that. To do so would be inauthentic. If you resonate with these words, then let's reject the shallow Big-Faced Worship and choose to live out our faith like the deep and weathered followers of Jesus he calls us to be.

Let's learn to carry our crosses daily, put Jesus first, and follow him with every aspect of our lives.

After all, that's what Jesus means when he calls us to follow him.

14

HAPPINESS VERSUS JOY

Another thing Big-Face Worship does is confuse Christians about what true happiness and joy are. I hope American Christians will stop confusing these two terms by thinking Christians should always be happy, and that if we're not always happy, then there's something wrong with us.

For example, if someone's brother dies in his sleep (like mine), then how can these kinds of misguided Christians think we should be happy about that? How can they think that if Christians aren't happy like they are, it's because we don't believe the gospel, or because we are doubting our faith in Jesus?

Instead, Paul says we should rejoice with those who rejoice, and mourn with those who mourn.[68] He also says we should grieve, but not like those without hope.[69] And again, if Jesus wept when he saw the devastation, grief, and sadness of his friends, Maria and Martha, when their brother Lazarus died, then how can we not be expected to weep with our friends, just like Jesus did?

In fact, since Jesus is the image of the invisible God in whom the fullness of the deity dwells bodily, then the tears of Jesus reveal to us the heart of God when we are hurting or suffering.[70] That means that just as Jesus's heart broke when he saw the grief and sadness of his friends, Jesus's broken heart and tears reveal to us the broken heart of God when his children go through similar things.

True faith embraces all of life, and calls us to bring our joys, good times, and happiness all to Jesus, as well as our tears, defeats, sadness, grief, and pain. He will take them all, and value them all, which means we don't need to cover up the hurtful, painful things as though they somehow undermine our faith in Jesus.

In fact, probably half of the 150 psalms are writings of lament about painful, hurtful experiences the authors are going through. They present them to God and ask him to move and help the person out of those difficult circumstances.

And if that were not enough, there's an entire book in the Old Testament called Lamentations, which is nothing but one huge lament about the harsh reality Israel, and the book's author, were going through.

Scripture recognizes, embraces, and values all of our human emotions and experiences. It calls us to lay them all at the feet of Jesus so he can help us through them, and hopefully move us to healing and restoration.

But Scripture never tells us to deny the painful things we go through.

And it never tells us that to acknowledge that pain means we lack trust or hope in God.

On the contrary, Scripture teaches us to lay our difficult circumstances and realities at God's feet by recognizing them, embracing them, and then asking him to help restore or heal us in that process. In fact, that is precisely what the authors of the Psalms do.

Therefore, in the rest of this chapter, I will explore what true happiness and joy are from the perspective of Scripture. I will do this so American Christians have a better understanding of what they are, and how we are called react and respond to them when they show up in our lives.

As I mentioned briefly in the section above, about two years ago, just after my wife Melanie and I got married, we realized I inherited Huntington's Disease from my dad. The symptoms of Huntington's Disease are very similar to those of Parkinson's. It involves lots of shaking and bodily movement that is beyond the control of the people who have it. The symptoms don't show up until later years, so I just started to see the initial signs of it.

The main difference is that the only way to get Huntington's Disease is by inheriting it from a mother or father. It's genetically passed on, whereas there are lots of possible causes for Parkinson's. Each child of someone with Huntington's Disease has a 50% chance of inheriting it form their mom or dad.

We had known for a number of years that my dad had it, which meant that all of us kids knew there was a 50% chance of us having it, too. But we didn't want to get tested, since there is no cure for it, and since none of us had blatant and obvious symptoms.

Then, shortly after getting married, Melanie and I found out I have Huntington's Disease, too. At first, I was pissed off and angry at God because I knew he could heal me but chose not to for whatever reason. From my time in ministry, I knew that while most people who go through things like that don't receive God's healing, there are some who do.

In fact, when I was serving with Youth with a Mission

(YWAM) in Argentina, I knew a girl from Southern California who God healed of fibromyalgia, which has no cure. The same guy who prayed for her also prayed for two friends, one from Peru and one from Puerto Rico, who were both HIV positive. God healed them both through this man's prayers, and to this day they don't have HIV or AIDS.

So, while I knew God can and does heal, I also knew that most often he doesn't answer those prayers for healing. Most of the times when we pray for healing, God doesn't heal, just as he never did during the thousands of times we asked him to heal my severely mentally and physically handicapped brother, Jonathan.

In fact, the reason we call those acts *supernatural* is because they go outside and beyond what is *natural*. When we get a sickness or disease in the natural world, it affects our bodies. In the natural world, without any interruption from outside of it, we are left to live with the consequences and symptoms.

So, when God occasionally intervenes and breaks that natural process, it is anything but natural. That's why we say it's *super-natural*, because it defies nature and goes beyond it. But that also means that, by definition, those supernatural healings are not the norm; they stand out as unusual precisely because they are unusual.

While we recognize that God can heal or answer our prayers —and we should at least give him that opportunity by praying for that—we should also realize that the normal, *natural* way of things is that, most of the time, God doesn't intervene.

While I had a number of people pray for me to be healed of my Huntington's Disease when we first found out about it, I came to realize that God wasn't going to heal me and that I would need to adapt my life to this new reality. This has not been easy, and it has taken the better part of two years to work through. In fact, I'm still very much in the process, but I make more progress every day.

I share this with you because a good friend of mine, who was a pastor and is a mentor figure for me, gave me a book, called *You Gotta Keep Dancin'*, to help me work through my anger, sadness, and grief at my Huntington's diagnosis. Years earlier, this same friend broke his back and had to recover over a period of about six months, and he said this book helped him regain perspective and hope after his accident.

The book was written by Tim Hansel, who was a ministry leader that fell while ice climbing, severely damaging his body and having to endure intense pain for the rest of his life. This book helped me regain perspective and my sense of faith and hope in God after my diagnosis. I want to use it to address the issues of happiness and joy in this chapter, and the Advantages of Disadvantages in the next chapter.

Tim writes this about happiness and joy:

The word happiness comes from the same root as the word happening, suggesting that happiness is based on something happening to us. Happiness is circumstantial. If I pay off my car, I'm happy. If I get a new shirt, I'm happy. If my friends say nice things, I'm happy.

There is nothing wrong with happiness. It's wonderful. The only problem is that it's based on circumstances, and circumstances have a tendency to shift. Most people who live with chronic pain or chronic problems have a hard time being happy. That is to be expected. Although there are moments of laughter, nothing seems to stay.

Joy, on the other hand, is something which defies circumstances and occurs in spite of difficult situations.

Whereas happiness is a feeling, joy is an attitude. A posture. A position. A place.... Joy is that deep settled confidence that God is in control of every aspect of my life.[71]

This is why the great ethicist Lewis Smedes says:

You and I were created for joy, and if we miss it, we miss the reason for our existence. . . . If our joy is honest joy, it must somehow be congruous with human tragedy. This is the test of joy's integrity: is it compatible with pain? . . . Only the heart that hurts has a right to joy.[72]

I love these words because they teach us what true happiness and joy are. Tim says happiness is based on our happenings, which always change. That's not good or bad. It's just reality. When good things happen to us, we're happy. When bad things happen to us, we're not happy.

But joy is like a deeply ingrained posture and attitude that shapes our whole life and reminds us that God has us in his hands. And according to the words of Hansel and Smedes, true joy helps us make sense of tragedy, and helps us walk through it.

The problem is that most Christians confuse joy and happiness.

They mistake happiness for joy, and therefore think that since we're called to be joyful, then we must be happy. So what do they do? They only laugh, smile, and show happiness, because they think something would be wrong with their faith if they actually showed and expressed the sorrow, grief, sadness, and pain they really feel.

When Christians and churches do this, we are left with entire churches that are based on this superficial Big-Face Worship.

When Christians think they need to be happy all the time because that's what it means to trust God, they fall in the trap of Big-Face Worship.

That shallow and triumphant worship and faith has nothing to say to us when we face real tragedy, grief, sorrow, pain, or loss.

But, as we've seen here, that's not what Scripture means when it calls us to be joyful.

It means we should have this attitude of joy even when we're not happy.

We should be able to have a certain deep trust in God even when we are going through pain, suffering, or anything that makes us unhappy.

I will never be happy about the painful things I had to endure during my life. Who would? I wish I never had to go through any of those things. But that doesn't mean I can't still be joyful about my suffering, because I know God has used it in great ways in the past, and that he is using it again now. After all, here I am writing books borne out of my trials and suffering, trying to give people hope and draw them closer to Jesus.

I will also never be happy about having an incurable disease like Huntington's Disease.

What kind of person would be happy? But just because I'm unhappy about that doesn't mean I can't still be joyful, because I'm learning to live life differently than I did before. I'm learning how to adapt to my new circumstances and still find joy, purpose, and meaning in living every day for Jesus.

The other thing Tim says in his book is that we must choose joy. It's a choice we need to make every day. Here are his words:

> It is not a feeling; it is a choice. It is not based on circumstances,
> it is based on our attitude. It is free, but it is not cheap. It is the

byproduct of a growing relationship with Jesus Christ. It is a promise, not a deal. It is available to us when we make ourselves available to him. It is something we can receive by invitation and by choice...

Pain is inevitable, but misery is not. We cannot avoid pain, but we can avoid joy. God has given us such immense freedom that he will allow us to be as miserable as we want to be.

I know some people who spend their entire lives practicing being unhappy, diligently pursuing joylessness. They get more mileage from having people feel sorry for them than from choosing to live out their lives in the context of joy.

Joy is simple (not to be confused with easy). At any moment in our life we have at least two options, and one of them is to choose an attitude of gratitude, a posture of grace, a commitment to joy."[73]

Joy is a choice.

It's so simple, and yet so hard sometimes to live out.

It's inevitable that we're going to have pain at some point in our lives, but misery is not inevitable. It all depends on how we choose to respond to these difficult situations.

For example, the Apostle Paul could have gotten very bitter and miserable when he was being whipped and arrested for proclaiming the gospel, but he didn't. Instead, he chose to have an attitude, a posture of joy. He knew that even if he had to suffer much pain and anguish, the Gospel was being proclaimed and increasingly more people were choosing to follow Jesus. He chose to override the unhappy circumstances of what was happening to him, and instead he chose to have a grateful attitude of joy.

Similarly, after I found out about my Huntington's Disease, I was so angry at God that I couldn't even go to church for about 6 months. But then I started to realize that I still have around 20–30 years until my symptoms get significant enough to where it will disrupt my daily functions. When I looked with that perspective, I began to see that I should be grateful for the years of health that I will still have.

I also discovered that doctors expect a cure for Huntington's sometime in the next 3-8 years, so my long-term outlook is very positive and hopeful.

I knew that none of us are even guaranteed that we'll make it to tomorrow, which I learned when my brother passed away in his sleep. So once again, if God gives me the grace to make it through one more day, week, month, or year, then I'll be grateful for the time I have.

And if I'm blessed enough to actually be alive in 30-50 years years, then I'll be even more grateful for the time God gives me.

This is what Hansen means when he says we must choose joy.

I'm still learning how to do this, but I've found these words to be very true and helpful, which is why I wanted to share them with you. My hope is that they will help encourage you to trust God in the midst of your pain and suffering, so you can learn to choose joy instead of bitterness, anger, and misery.

I've lived with bitterness and misery, and it's like being dead inside.

But when we realize true joy is not based on what is happening to us, like happiness is, then we are freed to walk through suffering, pain, and sadness while never losing sight of the joy and grateful attitude we choose to live by.

In fact, we can only experience joy to the same extent we experience pain and suffering. That's why I love the words from Lewis Smedes, when he says true joy must make sense of human tragedy and suffering, and help us walk through it.

If Christians continue to misunderstand what happiness and joy are, then we will continue to confuse them and think God calls us to be happy when we are experiencing personal tragedy, loss, grief, anxiety, fear, sadness, anger, or anything else.

But that is ridiculous.

No one, including me, is happy about those things.

We are called to have joy in those circumstances, but I hope that by now we know the huge difference between happiness and joy.

So, what are the things that are making you unhappy?

And how can you choose to find joy in those unhappy circumstances?

15

THE ADVANTAGES OF BEING DISADVANTAGED

When Christians live out the shallow, superficial Big-Face Worship, we end up denying or ignoring the inevitable pain, hurt, sadness, grief, and suffering we go through as a part of life. When we close ourselves off to those things, then, without realizing it, we also close ourselves off to what Tim Hansel calls "the advantages of disadvantages."[74]

These are things he has learned since his ice climbing accident, which forced him to reassess his life and live in a very different way. At first, he was angry at God, just like I was when I found out about Huntington's, but then he began to realize that he still had lots of great things he could do, and that he should be grateful for them.

This process helped him discover there were certain benefits, which he calls advantages, to the physical disabilities he had after his accident. These are things that are very hard for people without disabilities to learn, but which become the character, facts, and reality for people when they suffer from a disability or disadvantage.

Tim's words helped me a lot as I was trying to work my way through my own diagnosis of Huntington's Disease. I didn't know if I would still be able to live my life in a way that gave me purpose, fulfillment, or joy, and I was really frustrated and angry about my situation. Since reading this for the first time, I have discovered how true these words are, which is why I want to share them here:

> The big dream in our society is that if we work hard enough, we will eventually be able to experience a life without limitations or difficulties. It is also one of the biggest sources of friction in our society, creating disappointment, unnecessary suffering, and missed opportunities to live a full life. Some people spend their entire life waiting for that which will never, and can never, happen.
>
> Limitations are not necessarily negative. In fact, I'm beginning to believe that they can give life definition, clarity, and freedom. We are called to a freedom of and in limitations— not from. Unrestricted water is a swamp—because it lacks restriction, it also lacks depth. The conclusion we arrive at all depends upon how we look at our limitations.[75]

Tim says limitations aren't always negative, and some people spend their whole lives pursuing a life without limitations; but they are chasing after something that doesn't exist. Human beings are limited by time, space, and things like pain, food, water, people, and tons of other issues. Therefore, to be human means to live with limitations.

I agree that the dream of our society is to live without limits, but that's impossible for us. We are limited by things like our physical bodies, money, time, food, water, the actions of other people, our neighbors, our enemies, where we were born, and many other things.

And even Jesus was limited by these things.

He was a human being, limited by his physical body in a way he wasn't before coming to us as the person of Jesus. He was also limited by things like food, water, and other people. Even Jesus's own will was limited because he strove to do his Father's will, which wasn't always what Jesus wanted to do.[76]

Jesus found his true freedom in his own human limitations, not separate from them.

That means that, for us to be fully human like Jesus, we need to embrace our limitations and find freedom in them, not separate from them. We need to realize that none of us can live without limitations, and that even if we had everything else provided for us, we still wouldn't be free because we have given our lives to Jesus, which means he is our lord and master.

Breaking Through Our Superficiality

After making the point about limitations being good, Tim lists several other advantages of being disadvantaged, which we will go through and unpack so we can apply them to our lives. The first one has to do with the fact that pain and suffering break through our superficiality and force us to live on a deeper level:

> One of the greatest tragedies of our modern civilization is that you and I can live a trivial life and get away with it. One of the advantages of pain and suffering is that it forces us to break through our superficial crusts to discover life on a deeper and more meaningful level.

I recently found a simple but surprising sentence by St. Paul in II Corinthians 10:7, "You are looking only on the surface of things." Pain forces you to look below the surface. The tragedy is that many of us never have the courage to choose to do that. Hence we waste much of our life in bitterness and complaint, always looking for something else, never realizing that perhaps God has already given us sufficient grace to discover all of what we are looking for in the midst of our own circumstances.[77]

I love these words because, during the nearly seven years I lived in Latin America, I realized just how trivial and comfortable our lives are in the USA. The truth is that it seems like we can live a life just fine and never need to call on, or depend on, God. As a whole, we earn more than enough money from our jobs, so very few of us are in danger of not having shelter or food.

We can also buy everything we want at one huge store like Target or Walmart. In fact, I always say laughingly that if something isn't in Target, then it doesn't exist. We can buy everything we need with one or two stops. We also have refrigerators and freezers that can keep things for weeks or even months.

And since almost all of us have all this at our fingertips, it seems like we don't need God.

We don't depend on his provision for food, water, shelter, or clothes like the vast majority of the people in our world do, so we don't feel the need to depend on him.

As a result, we get lost in the trivialities and comforts of our lives.

But nothing breaks through that like pain and suffering.

And if your younger brother (like mine) was born severely handicapped, to the point where, during his 21 years he was never able to say one word, take one step, eat or drink on his own, use a bathroom, or move his hands, feet, or body in any way; then very quickly you realize life is fragile, hard, and beautiful, and that we should enjoy it while we can.

My younger brother Jonathan (Jono) taught our whole family that lesson.

Jono was 100% dependent on people to do absolutely everything for him, and it was so hard to have someone like that in our family. We loved and supported him for as long as we could, but after eight years, we couldn't handle it any more. He was getting too big for us to manage, and his medical needs were getting beyond our abilities to provide.

So when he was eight-years-old, but still had the functions and body control of about a 6-month baby, we decided to put him in a home where he lived the rest of his life. Having someone like Jono in our family shaped us all and taught us to appreciate the simple things in life.

It also taught us that life is fragile and none of us should take it for granted.

Jono also lived on raw emotions. He was incapable of any higher reasoning, so he responded to things emotionally like any 6–8-month baby does. He laughed if something was funny, and he cried when something made him sad, scared, or upset. That was the only way he could really communicate during his 21 years of life.

Jono taught us to embrace and express the ugly, hard, beautiful realities and emotions we were all living through. He taught us to celebrate and express things that are crazy, weird, strange, or funny, because that's how most of life is if we ever take the time to stop and notice.

Jono even taught us that lesson one more time when he passed away one night in his sleep. We didn't get a chance to say good-bye. Instead, one morning, he just didn't wake up. God used

Jono to bring me back to him when I was in my 20's. He is the constant reminder for our family that life is fragile and short, and that we should embrace all of it for the short time we're here.

I have also seen this truth expressed in the people of Latin America during my six and a half years there. While the people in Latin America as a whole are much more impoverished than the people of the USA, I would say that they are also way more joyful and happy than their filthy rich neighbors to the north.

Why is this?

How can poor Latin Americans be so much more happy and joyful than we are?

I think it's because the poor people of Latin America embrace their limitations and financial needs, so they appreciate life more than we do. Due to their suffering, pain, and dependence, they suck the marrow out of the bones of life.

They enjoy and celebrate life, even though it's hard.

We Americans may technically live longer, but we live in such a way that true meaning, fulfillment, joy, and purpose elude us.

That's not the case with our poorer neighbors to the south, who squeeze everything out of every day.

Helping Us Identify with Others

One of the other advantages of being disadvantaged is that it helps us connect with other people who are suffering:

> We live in a society that looks only on the surfaces. But pain, if allowed, produces identification with the suffering of others, and even with Christ, that we could not experience in any other way. One is allowed to see dignity in the midst of human struggle and see beyond the false barriers that are oftentimes

imposed between human beings. If our maturity grows, perhaps we even learn to see Christ in each other, and even in ourselves.[78]

This is so true. My little brother Jono taught my whole family to be sensitive to the needs of others, and especially of those with some kind of disability. We were all raised with that kind of compassion and sensitivity as the foundation of our lives. It shaped how we viewed and reacted to other people; and it helps us remember that we don't know what things people are dealing with at home, so we should give them the benefit of the doubt.

Appreciating the Little Things

Here is what Tim wrote about appreciating the little things in life:

> I realized again that I was blessed with a continual reminder that all of life is a gift and even the simplest acts and events are meant to be treasured. . . . My appetite for wonder has never been greater. My appreciation for so called ordinary things has never been richer. Perhaps I could have learned these things otherwise, but I think not. In my more honest moments, I realize that some things I thought I just had to endure were really special blessings meant to teach me how special life itself is.[79]

I have found these words to be very true in my life. When we have a disadvantage or disability, or when someone in our family does, we learn to see life differently than most people. For example, I have surfed my whole life and have pretty much taken it for granted until I got diagnosed with Huntington's Disease and couldn't surf for the past two years.

A big part of the reason I couldn't surf was because my muscles got fatigued so quickly that it was dangerous for me to be out in the water. So I stopped surfing two years ago when I got diagnosed, and just assumed I would never surf again, even though I live only 4 blocks from the beach.

But over the past 6–12 months, I realized that much of what my body was doing had nothing to do with Huntington's Disease. It was the result of other things. As I addressed those things, I felt better and better. I was even thinking about starting to surf again, although with a slightly bigger board in order to paddle easier.

Then I went to my last appointment with my doctor. He said I looked great, that my symptoms were decreasing, and that it was the result of a new medication I was on, as well as remedying all the other things going on in my body.

He also said I should start surfing again so I get exercise and begin to recover the things I stopped doing when I got diagnosed. In fact, he gave me orders to start surfing again, which was the best prescription I've ever gotten!

So after two years of living four blocks from the beach and not surfing at all, now I'm surfing again whenever there's waves, and I'm loving it. I use a bigger board so I can paddle faster. My muscles still fatigue a little faster than they used to, but I've also been out of the water for two years, so that's expected.

I tell you this because I used to take surfing for granted. I just assumed it would always be there. Of course, there were times when I didn't surf for six months or so, and other years when I rarely surfed because I was doing other things. But two full years is by far the longest I've ever gone without surfing.

I tell you this so you realize it wasn't until I was diagnosed with Huntington's Disease, and had to stop surfing for what I thought would be forever, that I really appreciated surfing. And since Huntington's took surfing away for two years, now I look at it completely differently.

I appreciate it so much more.

I realize it's a gift from God.

I also realize surfing isn't my right, but rather a blessing from God that can be taken away at any moment.

So every time I go out, I thank God for letting me surf. I ask him to keep me safe. I also ask him to help me connect with other surfers out there so I can get to know them, hopefully getting to influence them in some way.

Then, before I walk the four blocks to our apartment, I sit on one of the concrete benches and just watch the waves for a while.

I take in the sun.

I take in the morning breeze and stillness.

I take in the swell and the surfers, as well as the greens and blues in the water.

Before getting Huntington's and having surfing taken from me, I never did any of those things. I just surfed, and most of the time it was for my own benefit. I tried to stay away from people and keep quiet in the lineup. Now I look for people and talk with them out there.

I rarely ever used to pray before going out, either. In fact, I used to do it only when the waves got really big. Now I do it all the time. I also never used to sit around and watch the surfing or waves afterwards. I used to just finish and leave ASAP to get on with whatever else I was doing that day.

I share this with you so you can see how my Huntington's Disease has made me appreciate the ordinary and everyday things so much more than I used to. This is how I've learned to appreciate the little things.

Teaching Us to Focus

When I was younger, I lived under the premise that I should have as many options open to me as possible. These options, or possibilities, were like paths or doors I could take that would lead me towards my future. There's certainly nothing wrong with having many doors and possibilities open to us, but I developed a very unhealthy habit regarding them.

My life was like a huge circular room with all kinds of doors that represented new possibilities, and each new possibility led down a hallway that represented new life experiences, which I could take if I wanted. I used to love having options and possibilities open to me, but I ran into a problem.

Any time I tried to choose one of these doors of possibilities, and walk down it to see where it led, I would get scared that I had to say good-bye to all the other possibilities and doors that were open to me. That fear and panic would cause me to run back into the same room I had been in before, where I could see all my potential life-paths and doors.

That left me living in the same place I had been before: with all these potential doors and life-paths that represent endless possibilities and potential, but without enough courage to choose one path and commit to taking it wherever it led me. I was paralyzed and began to watch life pass me by.

Here are Tim's very pertinent words about this very subject:

In a world that inundates us with choices, one can become disoriented and almost overwhelmed by too many options. Life can become thinned out by trying to do too many things. One of the advantages of disadvantages is the privilege of being forced to see that which is closer, that which is simple, that which has been given to you. Life must have limitations in order to have depth . . . What we have traditionally perceived as limitations are sometimes the lens which can bring out life into deeper and finer focus.[80]

Having someone who was so severely mentally and physically disabled like my younger brother often makes the obvious and easiest option the default. With his needs, life gets way clearer and simpler. It's not easy, because it's the hardest thing in the world to care for someone like that; but it is simple, for the reasons Tim states.

We choose the easiest, most obvious option, and don't waste time pondering anything else.

We don't have time or energy to think about anything else.

But with my Huntington's, which is not as severe as Jono's condition, I'm still limited and don't have as much strength and stamina as I used to. That means, once again, life gets simpler, and now I choose the obvious or easiest option.

Life isn't easy.

It's actually much harder than it was before. I just can't do what I used to do, so that eliminates lots of options.

But now it's simple, and I don't waste energy worrying about what I could be missing out on; I just make the most of what I have.

Trusting in God's Strength

Trusting in our own strength instead of trusting in God's strength is something we're all guilty of:

Time and time again, throughout both the Old and the New Testament, God expresses his desire to give us his genuine strength and power. Paul reminds us that one of the greatest limiting factors to receiving that power is our temptation to rely on our own strength.

> Most of my life, my energy and strength has been based on talent, effort, pushing, and striving. I spent much if not most of my Christian life thinking about what I could do for Jesus, rather than what he could do in me. Perhaps it is by God's grace that I'm no longer able to do all those things, but must learn a new kind of receptivity, a new kind of residing power, another kind of strength from a source which is not my own. In letting go—because I had to—I've discovered a more permanent kind of eternal peace and power.[81]

I really identify with Tim's words here. Most of my life has been based on me pursuing things on my own talent, effort, pushing, striving, and pulling. In fact, those words could describe me as a Christian, too. I constantly focus on what I can do for Jesus, instead of what he can do in me.

In fact, I think this is true of just about everyone in ministry. Our greatest temptation is to think God needs us to accomplish his will, when the truth is God doesn't need any of us, and we are completely expendable.

He is more than capable of carrying out his will without our help.

And the sooner we learn that lesson, the better our relationship with him will be.

The truth is that we trust in our own thinking, reasoning, effort, and strength. But the apostle Paul says our own strength is the thing that gets in the way of us letting God use his strength and power. It goes against everything we are taught as Americans: that we can do anything...but the truth is we can't.

We can't change peoples' hearts.

Only God can.

We can't draw people to Jesus.

Only God can.

We can do everything we can to facilitate that effort by our words and actions, but at the end of the day, only God can open someone's heart to him. We need to drill this truth through our heads.

When we start to operate and depend on God's strength and power, instead of our own, we will discover a source that is infinitely stronger than ours. When we depend on his words, instead of our own, we'll likewise discover a source that has infinitely more power to change people than does our own.

Our strength will eventually, inevitably, let us down; but God's strength never will.

Choosing Forcefully

Tim talks a lot about *choosing*. I think this is because it becomes such a foundational part of the lives of those of us who have disabilities:

Paul Tournier says that perhaps the most powerful and unused gift from God is choice. For me, a big step in maturity was letting go of the fantasy of some magical cure and beginning to understand that pain can either integrate or disintegrate me. The choice is up to me.

Pain is teaching me to choose more forcefully, more boldly. I'm learning how to say no with more aggressiveness, sometimes because I simply have to. I'm learning how to say yes with more honesty and openness because my life has become more vulnerable. The root of the word decide means "to cut." Perhaps one of the advantages of disadvantages is the fact that we have to cut. We have to make choices which we didn't have to make at earlier stages in our life.[82]

With a severe disability like my younger brother, these kinds of choices are clearer, more straight-forward, and simpler. With him, there were so many things we couldn't do. That doesn't make life easier, but it does make our decision process more simple and obvious.

But with my Huntington's, this has been different. More than anything else, I feel tired and fatigued, but I never know for sure if it's Huntington's or just me being tired. Most of the time, it's probably a combination of the two, but this means I can still do most of the things I used to do. In fact, there's actually very little I can't do because of my Huntington's.

But since my main symptom is fatigue, I can, technically, still do most the things I used to do; but when I try to do them all at once like I used to, that's when I feel tired. But then again, I'm 39 years old and will be 40 in about six months, so maybe my fatigue is a result of my age, too.

Because of this, I'm learning to say *no* more forcefully, and *yes* more openly and honestly. Sometimes my *yes* is more like a: *yes, but we'll have to see how it goes.* And when I get too tired or fatigued, I need to rest. My *no* is more forceful because it has to be. And if people get frustrated about that, then that's just the way it has to be. I'm frustrated, too, but I no longer have the energy to try to please them.

When people don't have these limitations, they often try to please everyone by doing whatever everyone wants. They try to say *yes* to everyone and everything, but that leaves us running around like crazy, trying to meet everyone's expectations. When we have these limitations, we have to protect ourselves. We know we can't please everyone, and we don't have the energy or strength to please everyone even if we wanted to.

16

CONCLUSION: WHAT WOULD JESUS THINK OF US?

In Part 1 of this book, I showed you the two ways of interpreting the verses that clearly teach that Jesus was not all-powerful or all-knowing.

The first view—which is, unfortunately, the view of most American Christians—takes beliefs about God being all-knowing (omniscient) and all-powerful (omnipotent), and then directly applies them to Jesus as if he had the same knowledge and power he had before he became a human being.

Because of this mistaken belief, they view passages that show Jesus's human limitations as threats to his divinity. They also try to ignore, hide, deny, or explain away all the verses that clearly show Jesus's human limitations, because those sections of Scripture threaten their misguided beliefs on this issue.

The second view, called the *kenotic view*, is named that because it is based on the Greek word Paul uses in Philippians 2:5–11 to describe Jesus *emptying* himself. This view says that Jesus emptied himself to become a human being, and then implies that he must have emptied himself of the very things he had when he was in the form of God before, like being all-knowing and all-powerful.

Because of this, the human limitations on Jesus don't cause any problems, nor do they contradict the belief in the divinity of Jesus. Instead, they show us how much Jesus emptied himself of things like his diving power and knowledge when he took the form of a human being.

That also means we can look to him to see how we should live our lives, since he was operating with the same set of human characteristics, attributes, and limitations that you and I live with daily.

What Would Jesus Do?

In light of everything we have gone over in this book, I think one of the many questions we should ask ourselves is: *what would Jesus do?*

In light of everything we said about Jesus emptying and humbling himself in Philippians 2:5–11, and how we see this self-emptying and humbling in the ministry and person of Jesus, what would Jesus do if he were in our shoes? In light of the fact that Paul says we should have the same attitude, or mind, of Jesus, then *what kinds of things would Jesus do* if he were alive today?

In this short chapter, we will answer that question by noting commonly accepted practices of American Christianity to show how they contradict the teachings and example of Jesus.

First: If Jesus were alive today and in our country, he would choose to live a humble life of serving and loving others instead of chasing the upward trajectory of the American dream. Please don't get me wrong; I think he would be okay with our upward movement and success if we do it in a way that builds people up and cooperates with them, but I don't think he would tear them down just so he could be number one.

If we dedicate ourselves to collaborating for a better future, of if we work with companies that are committed to creating a better future, then I think Jesus would encourage that.

I also don't think Jesus would compromise on who he works for, and what he did for work. For example, I know many Christian engineers who work in the aerospace industry. Now, I see no problem with this if they work on things like the space program at NASA, or in areas like putting weather satellites into orbit. These are completely peaceful means that I don't think Jesus would have any problem with.

But I don't think Jesus would work in that industry if he were forced to develop technologies for fighter planes or weapons that will be used to kill the same people Jesus emptied and humbled himself to serve and save.

Second: Jesus would push for a faith that embraces hardship and doesn't hide suffering. Jesus wouldn't embrace the Big-Face Worship that so many American Christians and churches embrace. That kind of shallow, inauthentic faith only embraces and expresses happiness, smiles, and laughter, but it's a lie because life isn't always like that.

Sometimes life is really hard.

An authentic faith allows us to come to Jesus with everything we are feeling, which means it could be happiness and joy, but also tears, sadness, and pain. Authentic faith and worship embraces suffering and hardship as part of what it means to follow Jesus, since he calls us to follow him and carry our crosses daily.

Third: Jesus would emphasize programs that help people with disadvantages. I don't think Jesus would eliminate programs, like most white American Christians do, that help people survive, cope, heal, and recover when they are going through tough times of pain, sorrow, grief, or suffering. I'm talking about the way most white conservative Christians try to eliminate things like welfare and health insurance for parents and families who are barely able to make it.

If Jesus empties and humbles himself to meet us down in the midst of our own pain and suffering, then why do so many self-proclaiming American Christians refuse to do this with these kinds of people and programs? We need people to work with the government to care for these people, since there are too many of them for any one sector of society to do it alone.

If we dare to take the self-emptying and self-humbling nature of the humanity of Jesus seriously, then we should embrace these areas of pain, grief, sadness, and suffering, and do everything we can to help people through them.

That means that, instead of fighting to eliminate these programs that help people, we should be fighting to expand them. It means we should be the ones trying to ease the anguish, pain, and suffering of these people by expanding things like welfare, food stamps, healthcare, Medicare, and benefits for seniors.

Helping the disadvantaged, in as many ways as possible, is what every follower of Jesus should be fighting for.

Fourth: Jesus would spend more time living out the message of scripture, and less time studying it. I don't think Jesus would spend as much time as most Christians do *studying* scripture. Let me explain this statement, since I can already hear my protestant and evangelical readers gasping for breath and fainting!

I don't think Jesus would spend so much time studying scripture, because I think he would focus more on putting it into action.

American Christians spend so much time studying scripture, memorizing it, teaching and preaching about it, but we forget the most important part about it: *doing it.*

For example, no amount of studying Greek or Hebrew is going to teach you how to forgive someone who just harmed you or your family, but that's what Jesus calls us to do.

Now, I went to seminary and have studied extensively, and I love it. In fact, I wouldn't be writing books now if that weren't the case. But I also stopped memorizing scripture years ago, because I was coming across all kinds of Christians who could memorize and recite hundreds of verses, but they didn't do any of them.

They can tell you all about the verses that talk about God's love, but they don't actually love people with their lives and actions.

Similarly, they can talk about theological points for hours, but they never put them into practice by interacting with the world Jesus came to reach and save. It's like my systematic theology professor Ray Anderson (who was a pastor for 40 years, as well as the guru of systematic theology at Fuller Seminary for about 40 years until he passed away) used to say: *if our theologies don't change our lives and actions in some way, then they're useless.*

True Courage

Jesus came to us as a real human being, with real human limitations. That means he wasn't like the superheroes we see in movies.

When an invincible superhero runs into a burning building to rescue people, it might look like courage, but it isn't. The superhero never put his life in any danger. He risked nothing of himself.

On the other hand, if a normal human being, like you or me, runs into a burning building to rescue everyone inside, that's very different. That person would be worthy of all our adoration because they risked their life to save us.

This is why we love firefighters so much.

In fact, I'm writing this on the 12th anniversary of the 9/11 attacks on the World Trade Center in New York, and the reason people everywhere still wear FDNY hats to support the Fire Department of New York is because those responders were the only ones who ran into the buildings to try and get as many people out as they could.

They had to suppress their will for self-preservation—or their desire to see their wives and children one more time—to run into those buildings that had been struck by the jets, and get as many people out as they could.

They laid their lives down so others could be saved.

And that is exactly what Jesus did for us.

Jesus saved us from being separated from God forever by laying his life down in our place. We can all enjoy eternal life with God, but only because he took on the suffering and death that we deserved.

If this is what Jesus did for us, then how else can we respond but with tears of joy, relief, gratitude, love, and appreciation?

How else can we respond to that breathtaking demonstration of love other than living our lives for the one who suffered and was crucified so we didn't have to be?

How else can we respond, other than by following the example of Jesus to empty and humble ourselves?

How else can we respond other than trying to reach and save the people who are still condemned to perish in the burning buildings of their lives?

Are you with me?

NOTES

1. Matt. 24:36; Mark 13:32.
2. Mark 5:25–34.
3. Matt. 26:39; Mark 14:35–36; Luke 22:42.
4. Luke 2:52.
5. Mark 6:4–6.
6. Craig Evans, quoted in Lee Strobel, *The Case for the Real Jesus,* (Grand Rapids: Zondervan, 2007), 61–62.
7. *Ibid.* 62.
8. Phil. 2:5–11, NRSV.
9. This is the same self-emptying and self-humbling from Philippians 2:5–11 that we saw last chapter.
10. Luke 1:26–35, NRSV.
11. Lev. 20:10.
12. Matt. 1:19.
13. Luke 2:1–7, NRSV.
14. Col. 1:15; 2:9, NRSV.
15. Phil. 2:5–11, NRSV.
16. Luke 2:52, NRSV.

17. Mark 5:24–34, NRSV.

18. Mark 13:32–33, NRSV.

19. Mark 14:32–36, NRSV.

20. Heb. 5:8, NRSV.

21. Mark 6:1–6, NRSV.

22. Heb. 2:14–18, NRSV.

23. Heb. 2:18, NRSV.

24. Luke 4:1–13, NRSV.

25. Luke 4:3, NRSV.

26. Luke 4:4, NRSV.

27. Deut. 8:3, NRSV

28. Luke 4:5–7.

29. Ps. 2:6–9, NRSV.

30. Luke 4:8, NRSV.

31. Luke 4:9–11.

32. Luke 4:12; Dt. 6:16.

33. Heb. 2:18, 4:15.

34. Luke 5:12–16, NRSV.

35. Luke 5:13.

36. Matt. 11:19; Luke 7:34.

37. 2 Cor. 5:20, NRSV.

38. John 11:35, NRSV.

39. Col. 1:15; 2:9, NRSV.

40. John 11:1–44, NRSV.

41. John 11:1–5.

42. John 11:4, NRSV.

43. John 11:21, 32, NRSV.

44. John 11:33, NRSV.

45. John 11:35.

46. John 11:4, 11, 12–15, 23.

47. John 11:33, NRSV.

48. Col. 1:15, NRSV.

49. Luke 13:33–34, NRSV.

50. *Messiah* is Hebrew for "God's anointed." The Greek translation is *Christos*, from which we get the English term *Christ*.

51. Luke 19:38, NRSV.

52. Luke 19:39–40.

53. Luke 19:41–44, NRSV.

54. Col. 1:15; 2:9.

55. John 13:1–20, NRSV.

56. John 13:1, NRSV.

57. John 13:3, NRSV.

58. Matt. 26:37–46, NRSV.

59. Matt. 26:38.

60. Luke 22:44, NRSV.

61. Mark 15:15, NRSV.

62. Mark 15:16–20. NRSV.

63. Mark 15:29–32. NRSV.

64. Phil. 2:5. NRSV.

65. Phil. 2:5–11. NRSV.

66. William Dyrness, *How Does America Hear the Gospel?*, (Grand Rapids: William B. Eerdmans, 1989.), 61–81.

67. 1 Thess. 4:13.

68. Rom. 12:15.

69. 1 Thess. 4:13.

70. Col. 1:15; 2:9.

71. Tim Hansel, *You Gotta Keep Dancin'*, (Elgin: David C. Cook, 1985), 53–54.

72. Lewis Smedes, quoted in Tim Hansel, *You Gotta Keep Dancin'*, (Elgin: David C. Cook, 1985), 53.

73. Hansel, *You Gotta Keep Dancin'*, 54–55.

74. *Ibid.* 93–109.

75. *Ibid.* 94.

76. Matt. 26:36–46.

77. Tim Hansel, *You Gotta Keep Dancin'*, 96.

78. *Ibid.* 100.

79. *Ibid.* 101.

80. *Ibid.* 102.

81. *Ibid.* 103.

82. *Ibid.* 104.

ABOUT THE AUTHOR

I grew up in a Christian family but turned my back on God when I was 11 or 12. Shortly after, I got into partying and lived like that until coming to faith at 22.

My younger brother Jonathan was severely mentally and physically disabled. Jono could never say one word, take one step, sit, stand, walk, crawl, feed himself, roll over, or do anything for himself. After years of caring for Jono, we had to put him in a home where he lived until he died at 21.

I turned away from God, partly because of unanswered prayers for Jono, but God also used Jono to bring me back to him. My dad's words at Jono's funeral sum up our feelings: "I would never wish for someone like Jono even for my worst enemy, but I would never let anyone take away the experience of having him." We rarely talk about Jono because, when we do, we cry. He is the lens I see through. He shaped all my views about God, faith, suffering, pain, sorrow, joy, and meaning. He's also my reminder that, one day, all things will be made new.

After coming to faith in college, I devoted myself to reaching the skaters, surfers, and partiers I grew up around. Eventually I lived in Latin America for 6.5 years, and helped plant a church dedicated to reaching Chile's skaters, surfers, and young people. Since returning from Chile in 2014, I married Melanie, which was the best decision I ever made.

To find out more about me, please visit www.greghaugh.com.

THANKS FOR READING!

If this book has been helpful to you, a quick, honest review (which you can do on Amazon in less than a minute) will help more people discover this book. I'd love to hear your stories of how it has impacted you and your feedback will help me improve my future books.

WANT TO STAY UP-TO-DATE WITH MY NEW BOOKS?

Join my newsletter for great articles and behind-the-scenes looks at upcoming books. You'll also get instant access to my e-book *Bumper Sticker Theology*, where I share the faith lessons we can all learn from bumper stickers. It's a good one! To join, please visit www.greghaugh.com/join.

Made in the USA
San Bernardino, CA
04 January 2018